I Sing to My Savior

New Hymns from the Stories in the Gospel of Luke

Carolyn Winfrey Gillette

All scripture quotations, unless otherwise noted, are from the New Revised Standard Version of the Bible. New Revised Standard Version Bible,Copyright © 1989 the Division of Christian Education of the National Council of the Churches of Christ in the United States of America. Used by permission. All rights reserved worldwide.

Cover design by Taylor Miller

ISBN: 9798840436646
Imprint: carolynshymns

Dedication

This book is dedicated to my husband Bruce—
my love, and my partner in life, family and ministry.
Bruce has encouraged me in my hymn writing—
making suggestions for new hymns, getting into good
theological and biblical discussions with me, and sharing
my hymns online.

These last two and a half years, Bruce has been
recovering from a bone marrow transplant for acute
leukemia— while serving a wonderful congregation,
working hard to care for creation, encouraging me in my
writing— and bringing me much joy in our life of faith
together.

Thank you, Bruce, for the life we share!

Love,
Carolyn

A Note of Appreciation

Thank you also to my brother, David, who originally
worked with us to develop my website of hymns and who
has managed it through the years:
www.carolynshymns.com I am also grateful to David for
his help in proofreading this book. Thank you!

Contents

Introduction and Hymn Use Permission

My favorite gospel is the Gospel of Luke, and one of the readings in Luke that I love the most is Mary's Magnificat in Luke 1:46-55. Some Christians who use a daily prayer book read the Magnificat (along with Psalms and other scriptures and prayers) every evening. Here, young Mary sings out her praise to God and rejoices that God is active in this world. God is here among us! God loves and saves ordinary people!

Mary uses wonderful words to describe God's powerful and merciful work:

God has looked with favor…
God has done great things…
God has shown strength…
God has brought down the powerful…
God has lifted up the lowly…
God has filled the hungry…
God has sent the rich away empty…
God has helped God's servant Israel…
God has kept promises made through the generations.

God is not one who sits idly by. God loves this world, and God showed that love, in its fullness, in Mary's son Jesus— a gift to the whole world. It's no wonder she sang a song!

We see God's active love not only in the Magnificat; it is clear throughout Luke's gospel.   God's salvation— which can be described as healing and wholeness on so many different levels— is for everyone, including the people who, too often, are oppressed, avoided, looked down upon, excluded from the party, and judged by others.

We live in a world where hurting, struggling people desperately need to be reminded that they (we) are not alone. God is with us. God continues to be active in history. If we were writing a song of praise to God today, we might choose different, wonderful words:

God gives curiosity and knowledge to scientists…
God welcomes refugees and immigrants at the borders…
God fills youth with courage to speak out against gun violence in their schools…
God gives young people and old people the energy to work hard to counter climate change...
God walks beside each foster child who is being taken to yet another temporary home…

God stays by the bedside of the 90-year-old woman who is dying of Covid…

God welcomes people who are pushed aside…
God gives vision to church leaders…

God gives creativity and compassion to social workers who are helping homeless families…
God gives patience, strength and the joy of teaching to first grade teachers in inner city schools…

God gives persistence and vision to community organizers who are encouraging our nation to be just and merciful…
God works through those in law enforcement and government who are seeking to serve with integrity and work for the common good…
God gives sensitivity and love to teachers of children with special needs…
God helps parents who are at home nurturing their children…
God walks with people who quietly volunteer in their churches…

God gives faith and creativity to musicians who play and sing songs of praise, love and justice…

God gives wisdom to immigration attorneys…
God walks beside the people who are victims of violence and war…
God comforts the victims of abuse…

God fills us with words and actions to help bring an end to injustice…
God helps rich people learn the emptiness of putting their ultimate hope in money…

God continues to cast down the mighty from their thrones and to lift up the lowly.   God is at work in the world— through ordinary, faithful people.

Hymns are prayers that are sung, often in the community of a congregation, but also during personal times of prayer, Bible reading and reflection. Many hymns are directly based on specific scripture readings, and quite a few of mine are based on the stories found in Luke's gospel.

At the same time, these hymns include the joys and sorrows of the world we live in. They are prayers to God— to the One who continues to love, nudge, call, guide, challenge, strengthen and forgive us in our world today.

I have been writing new hymn texts to familiar hymn tunes since 1998, and I have been serving as a pastor during this entire time. Thank you to all who have supported my hymn writing, prayed for me, suggested new hymn topics, bought my books, given my books as gifts to others, invited me to do workshops and seminars, shared in conversation with me about hymns and faith, sent me emails telling me about your churches, and encouraged me along the way.

I hope these new hymns enrich your personal times of devotion and prayer. Maybe you will sing them in your home or share them with family or friends. If you don't know the hymn tune for a particular hymn I have written, you can look up the hymn with its tune as a MIDI file at www.carolynshymns.com

Every hymn I have written has a tune name with it, and you can also identify the tune because I list a common, well-known hymn that is written to each one (for example: "AURELIA 'The Church's One Foundation'"). If you are not a musician, you might try playing the tune and singing along. Or, you may simply wish to read these hymns as poems and prayers.

With each hymn, I have included the accompanying scripture reading and also a brief personal reflection. There are also questions for you to ponder as you reflect on your own faith and life in the church, community and world. Maybe you will put this book on your table and read and reflect on a hymn each day.

Or, maybe you would like to use some of these hymns in worship at your local church. If you have purchased this book, you have permission to reprint one hymn of your choice in your worship bulletins or on screens for congregational use in worship, for a single-event/single Sunday use.

If you would like to use these hymns more regularly in worship, please consider supporting my hymn writing ministry:

Some churches request free use because they are small, struggling congregations that don't have music budgets or any other reasonable way to pay for hymn use. If this truly describes your church, you are welcome to reprint hymns for free, one-time use in your worship. Please include the proper copyright and contact information with the hymn. Please contact me at carolynshymns@gmail.com, tell me that you bought this book, that your church is struggling, and that you are using one or more of these hymns for free. I find it helpful to know which hymns are being most used by churches. Please find ways to support my hymn writing by sharing my hymns with pastors, church musicians and others.

Other churches have the resources to pay for hymn use, or they have someone who would be interested in "sponsoring" a hymn for use in worship— or they would simply like to support my hymn writing ministry. If this describes your situation, I would welcome a contribution for hymn use. You can give in one of two ways: You can make a PayPal contribution to me. Or, you can use my current postal mailing address. More information on these options is found on my website that contains over 400 hymns, all to familiar tunes: www.carolynshymns.com

I welcome hearing your ideas for new hymns, and I would be happy to talk with your church if you would like to commission a hymn.

My husband Bruce and I are serving a small congregation in the Southern Tier of New York State (close to the Finger Lakes). After leaving larger churches, we came to this wonderful, faithful congregation of God's saints so we could continue to serve together. Also, Bruce hoped to have some time to work on creation care issues for churches and I wanted more time to write hymns. We are grateful for the added income that comes from those who use my hymns and contribute for their use.

I enjoy hearing from people who are using my hymns in worship. Please consider dropping me an email at carolynshymns@gmail.com and letting me know which hymns you are using. Please let me know where you have found my hymns (in this book, on my website, in a church bulletin, etc.). I would love to learn more about your congregation— where your church is located and how you are serving God faithfully in these challenging times.

Blessings on you and your congregation as you sing to our Savior, and as you let your community know that God is active in this world.

God has called all of us to work together to bring wholeness, healing, love, and justice to people who— like many of the people in Luke's gospel— know what it is like to be on the outer edges of their communities and who feel the joy of being invited into God's reign.

Let us pray for each other and our ministries.

Grace and Peace,
Carolyn

Chapter 1

Read Luke 1:26-38 (New Revised Standard Version):

26 In the sixth month the angel Gabriel was sent by God to a town in Galilee called Nazareth, 27 to a virgin engaged to a man whose name was Joseph, of the house of David. The virgin's name was Mary. 28 And he came to her and said, "Greetings, favored one! The Lord is with you." 29 But she was much perplexed by his words and pondered what sort of greeting this might be. 30 The angel said to her, "Do not be afraid, Mary, for you have found favor with God. 31 And now, you will conceive in your womb and bear a son, and you will name him Jesus. 32 He will be great, and will be called the Son of the Most High, and the Lord God will give to him the throne of his ancestor David. 33 He will reign over the house of Jacob forever, and of his kingdom there will be no end." 34 Mary said to the angel, "How can this be, since I am a virgin?" 35 The angel said to her, "The Holy Spirit will come upon you, and the power of the Most High will overshadow you; therefore the child to be born will be holy; he will be called Son of God. 36 And now, your relative Elizabeth in her old age has also conceived a son; and this is the sixth month for her who was said to be barren. 37 For nothing will be impossible with God." 38 Then Mary said, "Here am I, the servant of the Lord; let it be with me according to your word." Then the angel departed from her.

Angel Gabriel Went to Galilee
SHOWALTER 10.9.10.9 with Refrain ("Leaning on the Everlasting Arms")

Angel Gabriel ... went to Galilee ...
Into Nazareth, a back-woods town —
"You're God's favored one! You will bear a Son."
See God's blessings come a-tumbling down!
Mary wondered: "How could this be?" It seemed so odd.
Came the answer: "Nothing, nothing is too hard for God."

Angel Gabriel ... said to Mary there ...
"Name him Jesus! He will be a king."
Mary, as she prayed, heard, "Don't be afraid."
See God's blessings and the joy they bring.
Mary wondered: "How could this be?" It seemed so odd.
Came the answer: "Nothing, nothing is too hard for God."

Angel Gabriel ... shared God's wondrous plan ...
"Old Elizabeth is pregnant, too!"
She's six months along! Go and sing the song:
"God is blessing me and blessing you!"
Mary wondered: How could this be? It seemed so odd.
Came the answer: Nothing, nothing is too hard for God.

God, we live in fear and we wonder here:
Are there blessings that still come our way?
When there's so much wrong, can we sing your song?
Can we see your love at work today?
God, we wonder: How can it be? It seems so odd!
Send your good news: "Nothing, nothing is too hard for God!"

Biblical Reference: Luke 1:26-38 Tune: Anthony J. Showalter, 1887
Text: Copyright © 2017 by Carolyn Winfrey Gillette. All rights reserved.
Email: carolynshymns@gmail.com
New Hymns: www.carolynshymns.com

Reflection - Angel Gabriel Went to Galilee

For several years, *The Presbyterian Outlook* editor Jack Haberer asked me to write sets of lectionary-based hymns for Advent and Christmas. This hymn for the Fourth Sunday of Advent, "Angel Gabriel Went to Galilee," was part of a set of Advent hymns I wrote in 2017. The final line of each verse is based on the angel's message to Mary: "For nothing will be impossible with God."

This is why I have hope as I look at the future. Nothing is impossible with God:

God is at work in each war-torn country— strengthening those who work for peace, justice, mercy and compassion…
God is at work in climate scientists and in ordinary people who want to better care for creation…
God is at work in people trying to provide life-saving medicine and research in a pandemic…
God is at work in family members who work for reconciliation during family struggles…
God is at work in compassionate people who welcome refugees and immigrants…
God is at work in loving families who welcome foster children…
God is at work in indigenous people who are water protectors, caring for God's earth…
God is at work in people who "put in a good word about Jesus" in their everyday conversations with friends…

In every situation where we see the possibility of change but dismiss it because we think the challenges are too great— where the land is too polluted, the powers and principalities are too unjust, or the future is too hopeless— the good news is that nothing, nothing is too hard for God.

—What are the things that seem impossible to you?
—Where have you seen God working to make impossible things happen?

Read Luke 1:39-55, including these words:

39 In those days Mary set out and went with haste to a Judean town in the hill country, 40 where she entered the house of Zechariah and greeted Elizabeth. 41 When Elizabeth heard Mary's greeting, the child leaped in her womb… (Luke 1:39-41)

Mary Gladly Told Her Cousin

IRBY 8.7.8.7.7.7 ("Once in Royal David's City")

Mary gladly told her cousin,
"Praise the Lord! My spirit sings!"
Young and humble, she'd been chosen!
God was surely changing things!
God of love, her words ring true
as we sing her prayer to you:

"Now my soul is gladly singing
at the greatness of the Lord.
I rejoice, for God is bringing
his salvation to the world.
All who live will say I'm blest
even in my lowliness.

"God is mighty, just and holy,
and he's done great things for me.
Those who fear him know the mercy
that God gives us endlessly.
Mighty ones are brought down low;
lowly ones find blessings flow.

"God has filled the poor and hungry,
and he's sent the rich away.
God is active here in history,
in a real and wondrous way.
God has promised, and I'm blessed,
for I know God's faithfulness."

Biblical Reference: Luke 1:39-56
Tune: Henry John Gauntlett, 1849
Text: Copyright © 2009 by Carolyn Winfrey Gillette.
All rights reserved.
Email: carolynshymns@gmail.com
New Hymns: www.carolynshymns.com

Reflection - Mary Gladly Told Her Cousin

This is another hymn that I did for *The Presbyterian Outlook*, I wrote some of them to Christmas carol tunes, at Jack's suggestion. Many people in churches love to sing Christmas carols during Advent; many pastors, musicians and worship leaders would rather sing Advent hymns during Advent and wait to sing Christmas carols during the Christmas season. So what would happen if I tried to write hymns for both groups of people— so people could sing the beloved Christmas carol tunes with words from the Advent biblical texts? My website has several years' worth of Advent hymns to Christmas carol tunes.

Take a look at the text itself and the wonderful story of Mary meeting Elizabeth that the beginning of the hymn celebrates. What is your experience of visiting people you love? The Covid-19 pandemic has forced many people to keep beloved family members and friends at a safe physical distance. There have been plenty of times when many of us have longed to hug grandchildren, children, nieces and nephews, and elderly parents. We have wished we could go out to lunch with friends for long conversations at the local diner. We have wanted to travel by bus, train or plane. At times, especially during pandemic surges (and as we have sought to care for the people we love who are immune-compromised) we have had to stay away.

Maybe we can appreciate all the more the wonderful meeting between the two cousins, old Elizabeth and young Mary. We can imagine Mary ducking through the doorway, stepping into the home of Zechariah and Elizabeth. We can almost see Elizabeth getting up, arms outstretched, with a smile and a look of love on her face. We can practically feel that sense of awe and wonder, as Elizabeth said, with her hand on her belly, "Oh, Mary, did you see that? I could see it and feel it! My baby is leaping for joy!

What a joy… what a blessing… you are the mother of my Lord!"

The two women shared a holy moment. "Mary Gladly Told Her Cousin" celebrates that moment, even as it moves forward with Mary singing her song of praise that we call The Magnificat.

—When have you gotten together with a dear friend or relative to share a good conversation about the important things that are happening in your lives?
—When have you been able to talk to someone about God's faithfulness to you and to your community?
—Is it ever difficult to have these conversations?
—What are the circumstances that make it easier to talk about these things?

Read Luke 1:39-55, including these words:

46 And Mary said,
"My soul magnifies the Lord,

47 and my spirit rejoices in God my Savior,

48 for he has looked with favor on the lowliness of his
servant.
    Surely, from now on all generations will call me blessed;

49 for the Mighty One has done great things for me,
    and holy is his name.

50 His mercy is for those who fear him
    from generation to generation.

51 He has shown strength with his arm;
    he has scattered the proud in the thoughts of their
hearts.

52 He has brought down the powerful from their thrones,
    and lifted up the lowly;

53 he has filled the hungry with good things,
    and sent the rich away empty.

54 He has helped his servant Israel,
    in remembrance of his mercy,

55 according to the promise he made to our ancestors,
    to Abraham and to his descendants forever." (Luke
1:46-55)

I Sing to My Savior
ASH GROVE 6.6.11.6.6.11 D ("Let All Things Now Living")

I sing to my Savior, for God has shown favor
on one who is lowly, of humble degree.
Now each generation, with great celebration,
will speak of God's mercy to people like me.
They'll pass on the story that God who is holy
Shows mercy to those who respect God's good ways.
Though times are distressing, I know of God's blessing.
My Spirit rejoices! I give thanks and praise.

I sing of God's power o'er those who devour;
God scatters the proud in the thoughts of their hearts.
God casts down the mighty and lifts up the lowly;
God offers us justice and hope and new starts.
God fills up the hungry, surrounds them with plenty,
and sends out the rich people, empty, away.
As God has long promised to save and to bless us,
So God walks beside us in love every day.

Biblical Reference: Luke 1:46-55
Tune: Traditional Welsh melody
Text: Copyright © 2018 by Carolyn Winfrey Gillette.
All rights reserved.
Email: carolynshymns@gmail.com
New Hymns: www.carolynshymns.com

Reflection - I Sing to My Savior

I wrote this hymn for Erin Schubmehl Jacobson at the time of her ordination; the Magnificat is one of her favorite biblical texts. I chose to set Mary's song to the joyful tune of ASH GROVE ("Let All Things Now Living"). We can imagine Mary's surprise at the angel's visit, her times of wondering what the angel's message meant for her and for the world, her concern about how her friends and neighbors would respond to her news, and her joy as she went to spend some time with her older cousin Elizabeth who was also expecting a child. Elizabeth greeted Mary with such warmth and love; it must have been a special time for both of them. The Magnificat expresses Mary's deep faith and her understanding that God was at work in the world and in her life— especially as God fulfilled the wonderful promise to send a Savior into the world.

Mary understood not only God's actions but also the ways of this world. She knew that, too often, people who have excessive power *get* that power by pushing others down as they climb to the top. Too often, their scramble to hold onto power drains the life out of people who have few physical, emotional, spiritual or financial resources in their lives. Mary also knew that God works in surprising and wonderful ways— turning the world upside down and bringing in God's reign.

Bruce and I pray the Magnificat regularly as part of our church's Wednesday evening Zoom prayer services that we have been doing every week since the beginning of the pandemic. We actually lead the prayer service twice each Wednesday evening— at 5:30 and 7:00 p.m. These gatherings have been a wonderful way for church members and friends to connect with each other for prayer, scripture reading, conversation and support. Our times of prayer with others have become a real gift during this pandemic, with all of its isolation and stress.

I hope that when you are reading this, the pandemic has become a less dangerous, less intrusive thing in your life and community— maybe even a distant memory. No matter how much it goes away in our society, it will remain an important part of our family story; we will always remember my 90-year-old mother's death from Covid, and Bruce and I will remember having to be very careful during the pandemic due to his recent bone marrow transplant. Every week, our two Wednesday prayer services come around again as times that strengthen our faith and to build community among our church members; every week, we read the words: "My soul proclaims the greatness of the Lord!" I celebrated Mary's faith that guides our own faith in the words of the hymn, "I Sing to My Savior!" What a wonderful prayer to offer as we begin singing through Luke!

—In the words of the hymn, who are the ones, and what are the things, that "devour"?
—How does God offer justice to people who are hurt by the mis-users of strength and might?
—How has God offered you "new starts"?
—How is God actively working in your life and community?
—What are the patterns of your praying times each day and each week? When and how do you sing praise to God?

Read Luke 1:39-55, including these words:

52 He has brought down the powerful from their thrones,
    and lifted up the lowly;

53 he has filled the hungry with good things,
    and sent the rich away empty.
(Luke 1:52-53)

My Soul Proclaims That God is Good

GREENSLEEVES 8.7.8.7 with Refrain ("What Child Is This?")

My soul proclaims that God is good
I sing to God my Savior.
For God has blessed me! I am loved!
God looks on me with favor.
God is not far away;
God cares for people every day.
God sees and loves the poor
And gives to them a blessing.

The Mighty One has done great things;
I see God's hand of mercy.
God's people know the love God brings;
They know that God is holy.
God is not far away;
God cares for people every day.
God sees and loves the poor
And gives to them a blessing.

God casts the mighty from their thrones;
The proud will surely scatter.
God lifts the lowly, hurting ones,
And shows them their lives matter.
God is not far away;
God cares for people every day.
God sees and loves the poor
And gives to them a blessing.

God fills the hungry with good things;
And sends the rich ones hungering.
God's promise was to immigrants
And also to their children.
God is not far away;
God cares for people every day.
God sees and loves the poor
And gives to them a blessing.

Biblical References: Luke 1:39-45; Luke 1:46-55
Tune: Traditional English melody
Email: carolynshymns@gmail.com
New Hymns: www.carolynshymns.com

Reflection - My Soul Proclaims That God is Good

I chose GREENSLEEVES as the tune for this particular hymn about Mary's Magnificat; we associate this tune with another song about Mary, "What Child is This?"

"My Soul Proclaims That God is Good" includes Mary's affirmation that God lifts up the lowly. In our world today, "the lowly" includes countless people who are fleeing violence and poverty in their homelands and trying to find safe places to live.

The year I wrote this hymn, 2018, was a hard year for immigrants and refugees in the United States. There were plenty of news stories about children and youth who had crossed the border and were being held by the U.S. government in detention centers; our government had brutally separated many of them from their parents. We heard from church workers about ten- and twelve-year-old children in detention centers, saying bedtime prayers with younger children and singing them to sleep at night, because these little ones had been taken away from the adults who loved them. The older children stepped up to help the younger ones as best they could. It was good they could still sing and pray, yet what a cruel way for a nation to treat vulnerable children!

While there have been some changes in national policy, there are still many challenges: understaffed immigration offices, long waits, and yes, children longing for parents who are still very far away.

As Mary sang her song of praise, she remembered how God had blessed Abraham and Sarah. We remember, too, that Abraham and Sarah were some of the many immigrants whose stories are told in the Bible. We pray that God's hand of mercy will bless immigrants today, including the children and youth.

—How can you work for immigration policies that "give to them a blessing" as God intends?
—How are your schools and local groups welcoming any immigrant children who may be living in your community?
—What is your church doing to help immigrants and refugees who are seeking safety and welcome?

Read Luke 1:57, 67-79, including these words:

78 By the tender mercy of our God,
the dawn from on high will break upon us,

79 to give light to those who sit in darkness and in the shadow of death,
to guide our feet into the way of peace (Luke 1:78-79)

When Old Zechariah Saw What God Had Done
MUELLER 11.11.11.11 ("Away in a Manger")

When old Zechariah saw what God had done,
He knew that the promised Messiah would come.
His speech was restored and his friends were amazed;
Recalling his words, we now offer God praise:

You've looked down with favor and rescued your own.
You've sent us a Savior from King David's throne.
The prophets once told us, "It's part of God's plan!"
And now we behold this: We're saved by your hand.

You keep what you promise and so we are blest;
In mercy you saved us when we were oppressed.
As Abraham heard you, we've heard your call too;
We're saved, so we'll serve you in all that we do.

We thank you, O God, that John pointed the way;
In Jesus our Lord now, we've seen your new day.
In Christ, the dawn brightens and death's shadows cease;
We'll live in your light and be guided in peace.

Biblical Reference: Luke 1:57-79
Tune: James Ramsey Murray, 1887
Text: Copyright © 2009 by Carolyn Winfrey Gillette.
All rights reserved.
Email: carolynshymns@gmail.com
New Hymns: www.carolynshymns.com

Reflection -
When Old Zechariah Saw What God Had Done

There are four Christmas songs at the beginning of Luke's gospel: Mary's Magnificat, Zechariah's Canticle, the song of the angels who proclaimed "Glory to God in the highest!" and Simeon's Canticle. "When Old Zechariah Saw What God Had Done" is a hymn that tells the story of one of these songs; it is the song of John the Baptist's father after John was born. Zechariah celebrates how God has kept important promises made many centuries before. The end of the reading and the end of the hymn both celebrate that the "dawn from on high shall break upon us," by the tender mercy of our God.

For several months, as Bruce and I were settling into the rural community where we now live, I worked at a job with the schools. I took this job as a way of helping children and also because I wanted to get to know our new community— all its hills and valleys, its back roads, its neighborhoods, its children and youth, and some of the very hard-working people who care for the children every school day. I rode a yellow school bus two times each day — securing wheelchairs to the bus floor, reading books to children on the 45-minute-ride to or from school, or simply chatting with little ones about home and school. In the winter, the morning bus runs started when the sky was still dark, and each day, we watched the sun rise over the hills and over the Susquehanna River as the bus wound back and forth on country roads.

On those bumpy sunrise bus rides, I often thought of these words of Zechariah: "The dawn from on high will break upon us." When the bus ride began each morning, it was so early that we could hardly see the turns in the road ahead, but as the sun came up, suddenly the roads were visible and safe. The dense morning fog in the river valley lifted.

The bus driver would turn up the radio station and play bright, cheerful morning music to wake everyone up a bit on their way to school. The sun shone bright, inviting us into a new day.

In John's birth, celebrated by his father Zechariah, and ultimately, in the birth of Jesus, God invites all of us into a new day with the gift of God's saving love. God seeks to give us wholeness— healing— in the physical, emotional, spiritual, family, community, national and environmental/ creation areas of our lives. God wants us to experience justice and reconciliation. So we move— walk, run, drive, ride— toward God's new dawn that is breaking upon us. Nothing can stop the coming dawn. Each new day is a gift from God. It's a new opportunity to know God's love and to respond to it. Each new day is a day to turn up the music and celebrate, as part of the community of God's people!

—What promise from God does this new day bring for you?
—How will you welcome it?

Chapter 2

Read Luke 2:1-20, including these words:

6 While they were there, the time came for her to deliver her child. 7 And she gave birth to her firstborn son and wrapped him in bands of cloth, and laid him in a manger, because there was no place for them in the inn.

8 In that region there were shepherds living in the fields, keeping watch over their flock by night. 9 Then an angel of the Lord stood before them, and the glory of the Lord shone around them, and they were terrified. 10 But the angel said to them, "Do not be afraid; for see—I am bringing you good news of great joy for all the people: 11 to you is born this day in the city of David a Savior, who is the Messiah, the Lord. 12 This will be a sign for you: you will find a child wrapped in bands of cloth and lying in a manger." (Luke 2:6-12)

O God, Your Grace Has Now Appeared
WINCHESTER OLD 8.6.8.6 ("While Shepherds Watch Their Flocks")

O God, your grace has now appeared
In Mary's tiny boy.
In this, your story, may we hear
Good news of wondrous joy.

Your gift of peace was heard that night
And shepherds were amazed.
Like them, may all your church delight
In angels' songs of praise.

As Mary and as Joseph heard
What shepherds came to say,
May we find wonder in your word —
For still you speak today.

God, by your Spirit, may we find
In words we've long confessed,
Your grace that calls us to respond —
To live as we've been blessed.

Biblical Reference: Luke 2:1-20
Tune: George Kirbye, in Thomas Este's *Whole Book of Psalms*, 1592
Text: Copyright © 2010 by Carolyn Winfrey Gillette. All rights reserved.
Email: carolynshymns@gmail.com
New Hymns: www.carolynshymns.com

Reflection - O God, Your Grace Has Now Appeared

The story of Christmas starts with God's gift of grace. We haven't done anything to earn it or deserve it. God simply gives us a gift— the gift of Jesus, the gift of God's love living among us.

Sometimes we aren't sure if the grace of God is for *us*. We may feel like an abused child whose spirit has been beaten down. When that little one is finally in a new foster or adoptive home with new, loving parents, she may be suspicious of the love she is offered. She tests boundaries to see what it will take for the new parents to stop loving her. She is sure it will happen; she wants to know her new parents' breaking point! Or, she makes mistakes and then cringes, waiting for her new parents to get angry and finally send her away. Yet the parents keep on loving her, and finally she can settle down and feel their gift of love surrounding her. So God— like a persistent, loving parent — keeps on loving us. That is grace.

The grace in the Christmas story calls for our response. God calls us to hear this old, old story with an ever-new sense of joy— to delight in the angels' message, to find wonder with the shepherds, and to respond with faithful obedience to Jesus' way of love. "O God, Your Grace Has Now Appeared" ends with the affirmation that God has blessed us in order that we may be a blessing to others.

—Where have you seen God's gift of love, freely given, in the world around you?
—Have you ever tested God's love?
—How and when have you accepted gifts of grace (from God or from others) when they come your way?
—How can you pass on this gift by showing God's grace to someone else today?
—Who, in your church or community, needs to experience unconditional love, freely given?

Read Luke 2:15-19, including these words:

15 When the angels had left them and gone into heaven, the shepherds said to one another, "Let us go now to Bethlehem and see this thing that has taken place, which the Lord has made known to us." 16 So they went with haste and found Mary and Joseph, and the child lying in the manger..." (Luke 2:15-16).

Also read Matthew 2:1-12 - The Visit of the Wise Ones

When Mary Hugged Her Newborn Son

TALLIS' CANON 8.8.8.8 ("All Praise to Thee, My God, This Night")

When Mary hugged her newborn son,
She pondered all that God had done.
Could she know all her child would be —
The life he'd bring humanity?

When shepherds heard the angel's joy,
They went to find that baby boy.
Could they see there in Bethlehem
A friend to outcasts just like them?

When wise men came with gifts to share,
They saw young Jesus playing there.
Could they behold in one so small
God's gift most precious of them all?

God, make us faithful, humble, wise
To know that Jesus changes lives.
May we be open to the way
That he would change our lives this day.

Biblical References: Luke 2:19, 2:8-20; Matthew 2:1-12
Tune: Thomas Tallis, 1561
Text: Copyright © 2011 by Carolyn Winfrey Gillette. All rights reserved.
Email: carolynshymns@gmail.com
New Hymns: www.carolynshymns.com

Reflection - When Mary Hugged Her Newborn Son

Bruce and I have three children, all adults now. We also had a foster son— a preschool boy— for 19 months when our other three children were college-age or beyond. Now, we have several grandchildren. We have hugged all of them many times! When they were little, we sometimes wondered about their future as we were hugging them. What would our three biological children grow up to be and what would they do? Would our foster son go back to his family's home, stay with us, or go to another home? Now we wonder: What will the world be like, in the future, for our children and grandchildren?

We can imagine all the things that Mary "pondered… in her heart" about Jesus' birth. From the words of the Magnificat, we can see that Mary was a young woman of deep faith; she trusted in what God was doing. She knew God sent Jesus as the Savior— but what exactly would that mean? She was faithful, but she was human! She couldn't see all the details of her son's future. What are the things she wondered about?

What did the shepherds and the wise men understand about Jesus?   Much of the joy of the Christmas story is that ordinary people, humble people, hurting people, pushed-to-the-side people, can see that— in Jesus— God did not come as a mighty ruler with all the privileges of wealth and power; God came into the world very simply as one of us.

The wise men are not in Luke's story, of course, yet they find their way from Matthew's gospel into our Christmas pageants and also into this hymn, "When Mary Hugged Her Newborn Son." They were outsiders in Bethlehem, too, finding their way to the baby sent from God. They were from a different place, a different culture. They remind us that Jesus is not bound by culture. God's gift—

most precious of them all— is for all people, in all times and places. They remind us that God reaches out to us wherever we are and makes us new people. So we pray, in the words of the hymn,

"God, make us faithful, humble, wise
To know that Jesus changes lives."

—What parts of the Christmas story remind you that Jesus came to be "one of us"?
—Mary, the shepherds, and the wise men all responded to the gift of Jesus and let their lives by changed by him. How does the gift of Jesus change your life today? How do you live differently because of Jesus' life, teachings, sacrifice, and love?
—When have you understood that God was working in a culture or religion that was not your own?

Read Luke 2:22-38, including these words:

22 When the time came for their purification according to the law of Moses, they brought him up to Jerusalem to present him to the Lord 23 (as it is written in the law of the Lord, "Every firstborn male shall be designated as holy to the Lord"), 24 and they offered a sacrifice according to what is stated in the law of the Lord, "a pair of turtledoves or two young pigeons."

25 Now there was a man in Jerusalem whose name was Simeon...

36 There was also a prophet, Anna... (Luke 2:22-25a, 36a)

A Baby, A Blessing! A Husband and Wife

ST. DENIO 11.11.11.11 ("Immortal, Invisible, God Only Wise")

A baby, a blessing! A husband and wife,
A prayer of thanksgiving for new human life!
New parents went up to the Temple to pray,
To offer their baby to God on that day.

A baby, a journey, two parents, two doves,
A gift humbly given in thanks for God's love!
An old man named Simeon rose to embrace
That wonderful baby, that sign of God's grace.

A baby — the One that the prophets foretold —
A woman named Anna, so wrinkled and old!
She praised God and told what this baby would bring;
She thanked God for letting her see such a thing.

A baby, a blessing, for all of us, too!
O God, we now offer our praises to you —
For we know the time of our waiting is done.
We've seen our salvation in Jesus your Son.

Biblical Reference: Luke 2:22-40
Tune: Traditional Welsh hymn, in John Robert's *Caniadau y Cyssegr*
(*Songs of the Sanctuary*), 1839

Email: carolynshymns@gmail.com
New Hymns: www.carolynshymns.com

Reflection - A Baby, A Blessing! A Husband and Wife

This hymn, set to the tune of ST DENIO ("Immortal, Invisible, God Only Wise"), celebrates the story of Simeon and Anna, whose lives were centered in the Temple. They had trusted God's promises for a long, long time. Finally, they were able to see God's promise of a Savior fulfilled when two parents came into the Temple with their baby. Simeon and Anna knew this child was special!

—When have you waited for God's help for a long time?
—When have you witnessed God's promises being fulfilled?

Mary and Joseph brought with them the sacrifice of two doves. This was the sacrifice to be offered to God by people who were poor (see Leviticus 5:7). Simeon and Anna had the wisdom to see God's salvation coming to the world through the poor family who stood before them.

—What does it mean to you that Jesus was born into a poor, humble home?
—How do you live differently, knowing that Jesus came from a family of modest means?

Read Luke 2:29-32:

29 "Master, now you are dismissing your servant in peace,
according to your word;

30 for my eyes have seen your salvation,

31 which you have prepared in the presence of all
peoples,

32 a light for revelation to the Gentiles
and for glory to your people Israel."

Lord, Let Your Servant Go in Peace
ST. PETER 8.6.8.6 ("In Christ There is No East or West")

"Lord, let your servant go in peace;
Your Word has been fulfilled."
Because we've seen your saving grace
We know that all is well.

Through all the sorrow, pain and death,
We dare, O God, to sing.
For you once sent your Son to earth —
And that changed everything.

There's much we cannot understand,
Nor order, nor control;
We place our lives into your hands
And trust you'll make us whole.

Lord, let your servants daily know
That we are not alone;
And may we find, where'er we go,
You'll lead us safely home.

Biblical Reference: Luke 2:29-32
Tune: Alexander Robert Reinagle, 1836
Text: Copyright © 2010 by Carolyn Winfrey Gillette.
All rights reserved.
Email: carolynshymns@gmail.com
New Hymns: www.carolynshymns.com

Reflection - Lord, Let Your Servant Go in Peace

I wrote this hymn for the Service of Witness to the Resurrection— the funeral service— for my mother-in-law; Simeon's canticle was a favorite scripture reading of hers. A few years later, my father died, and we used the hymn at his service. This past fall, we sang it at my mother's funeral, and this past fall, we also sang it at the long-delayed (because of the pandemic) service for Bruce's father.

All four of our parents were people of deep faith, and all of them lived into their 80's or 90's. Each one of them knew that, because of God's gift to us of Jesus Christ, "All is well." All of them held onto the hope of salvation.

Sure enough, they had tough times in their lives. They had seasons of "sorrow, pain, and death," as the hymn says. We have those seasons, too— and in those times, we "dare to sing." We dare to sing because God has given us a glimpse of the end of the story. It is as if our lives and our world are a book, and as we are reading the book, God lets us see what is happening on the last page. God wins! Love wins!   That's the ending that we see through faith-filled eyes, and it changes how we experience everything else along the way.

When Simeon and Anna were old and saw young Jesus in the Temple, they knew: God wins! Love wins!

When each of our parents died, they knew and we knew: God wins! Love wins!

When we have faced challenging times in our ministry, we knew: God wins! Love wins!

And that changes everything. We can live differently— more joyfully, more freely, more lovingly— in the present because we know the end of the story. We have faith that, in the end, God wins. Love wins.

—What is one hymn you remember from the funeral of a loved one? What special meaning did it have for you?
—When did you know, in the midst of tragedy, that, because of Jesus, all would be well?
—If you believe that God wins - love wins - how might you live differently today?

Read Luke 2:41-52, including these words:

41 Now every year his parents went to Jerusalem for the festival of the Passover. 42 And when he was twelve years old, they went up as usual for the festival. 43 When the festival was ended and they started to return, the boy Jesus stayed behind in Jerusalem, but his parents did not know it. 44 Assuming that he was in the group of travelers, they went a day's journey. Then they started to look for him among their relatives and friends. 45 When they did not find him, they returned to Jerusalem to search for him. 46 After three days they found him in the temple, sitting among the teachers, listening to them and asking them questions . (Luke 2:41-46)

Jesus' Parents Left the Temple

W ZLOBIE LEZY 4.4.7.4.4.7.4.4.4.4.7 ("Infant Holy, Infant Lowly")

Jesus' parents left the Temple with a traveling caravan.
They were sure their son was with them as they left Jerusalem.
Soon they cried, "We cannot find him!"
He was somehow left behind them,
So they went to search for him.

They went back and finally found him with the teachers of the Law.
What they witnessed was astounding! What a wondrous sight they saw.
For the questions he was raising
Showed his knowledge was amazing;
All who heard him were in awe.

Still his mother had to scold him, for she'd known a parent's fear.
"We were worried!" Mary told him. "when we could not find you near!"
Jesus answered Mary, saying,
"Did you not know I'd be staying
In my Father's house, right here?"

God of love, with earthly parents, Jesus listened, learned, and grew.
In the Temple, in your presence, he knew he was home with you.
We're reminded of his wisdom;
He already knew his mission
And the work that he would do.

Biblical Reference: Luke 2:41-52   Tune: Polish melody
Text: Copyright © 2015 by Carolyn Winfrey Gillette. All rights reserved.
Email: carolynshymns@gmail.com
New Hymns: www.carolynshymns.com

Reflection - Jesus' Parents Left the Temple

Here is a story that parents, grandparents, uncles, aunts, neighbors of small children and guardians can relate to. Have you ever felt the intense, immediate sense of fear after a child in your care wandered away into a crowd? Years ago, our family attended the "Stand for Children" rally in Washington, DC. At one point, we realized that our three-year-old daughter was no longer walking beside us. Where had she gone? We re-traced our steps— shouting her name— and finally we found her about a hundred feet back on the path we had just traveled. She had stopped to gaze up at the Capitol Police Horse Mounted Patrol, where uniformed officers were tending to their horses. We were so thankful to have found her! She thought nothing of it. She loved animals, and as far as she was concerned, she was comfortable where the animals were. What was more attractive to a three-year-old— a huge rally where people were speaking out for the rights of children— or a horse?

The biblical story of Jesus' in the Temple as a boy is one of the first stories that many children learn in Sunday School. While his parents were frantically searching for him, concerned for his safety, Jesus was where he knew he was supposed to be— engaging the religious leaders in conversation. This gives us a childhood hint of what was on Jesus' heart and mind— a life of obedience to God. The story also reminds us of the importance of being willing to ask questions about faith— and not to take things at face value. Sometimes when I was growing up, I heard people in church say, "The Bible says it, I believe it, that settles it." I was grateful to have parents who taught me to ask, "How?" "Why?" "Why not?" and "Are there other ways of understanding this? What are the deeper meanings?" We need to continue to teach the children in our lives to ask deep and searching questions— including questions about their faith.

We can start doing this when children are very young. One of my favorite story Bibles is *Growing in God's Love: A Story Bible* (Flyaway Books) by Elizabeth F. Caldwell and Carol A. Wehrheim. The authors are Christian educators who end each Bible story with three questions that call for a response, such as "What did you hear...? What did you see...? What will you do...?" I highly recommend this story Bible for families.

Adults and children can grow together when we talk about important things. Jesus' questions in the Temple surely gave the religious leaders something to think about, even as he grew in articulating his own beliefs. As we read the Bible, as we sing the songs of the church, and as we meet together to talk and to pray, we need to keep asking questions. They help us grow in faith, and they deepen our sense of calling.

—What faith questions have you asked recently?
—What faith conversations have you had with children?
—Who did you talk to about important things that matter?
—When has one of your faith questions helped you to get a better sense of what God is calling you to do?

Chapter 3

Read Luke 3:1-6:

1 In the fifteenth year of the reign of Emperor Tiberius, when Pontius Pilate was governor of Judea, and Herod was ruler of Galilee, and his brother Philip ruler of the region of Ituraea and Trachonitis, and Lysanias ruler of Abilene, 2 during the high priesthood of Annas and Caiaphas, the word of God came to John son of Zechariah in the wilderness. 3 He went into all the region around the Jordan, proclaiming a baptism of repentance for the forgiveness of sins, 4 as it is written in the book of the words of the prophet Isaiah,
"The voice of one crying out in the wilderness:
'Prepare the way of the Lord,
    make his paths straight.

5 Every valley shall be filled,
    and every mountain and hill shall be made low,
and the crooked shall be made straight,
    and the rough ways made smooth;

6 and all flesh shall see the salvation of God.'"

John Spoke As a Prophet
TO GOD BE THE GLORY 11.11.11.11 with Refrain

John spoke as a prophet, a voice to be heard.
He preached in the desert, proclaiming God's word:
"Come here and be baptized, and God will forgive!"
He taught all those people a new way to live.

Refrain:
God of truth! God of grace! Hear our cry and forgive!
May your church in this place find a new way to live.
Confront us and heal us, until we all learn
The life that is ours when we're willing to turn.

We hear in December a calling to shop;
We plan and we spend till we're ready to drop.
Our "wants" seem like "needs" when we enter a store,
Then outside we pass by the hungry and poor.
Refrain

We find that we're busy and weary each day;
We're worn and distracted, forgetting to pray.
It feels like we're walking on unsteady ground;
God, change us and mold us and turn us around.
Refrain

The valleys below will be filled to the brim,
The mountains above will be made low for him,
The rough, crooked ways will be made smooth and broad,
And all flesh shall see the salvation of God.
Refrain

Biblical References: Luke 3:1-6; Matthew 3:1-6; Mark 1:1-5
Tune: William Howard Doane, 1875
Text: Copyright © 2015 by Carolyn Winfrey Gillette.
All rights reserved.
Email: carolynshymns@gmail.com
New Hymns: www.carolynshymns.com

Reflection - John Spoke As a Prophet

The writer of the Gospel of Luke spends a significant amount of time talking about John the Baptist. Early on, Luke tells us the story that surrounded John's birth. Now we have the story of John as an adult, living in the wilderness, preaching and calling the people to be baptized.

Luke places this story of a prophet in a particular time and place in history: "…In the fifteenth year of the reign of Emperor Tiberius, when Pontius Pilate was governor of Judea, and Herod was ruler of Galilee, and his brother Philip ruler of the region of Ituraea and Trachonitis, and Lysanias ruler of Abilene, during the high priesthood of Annas and Caiaphas,.." (Luke 3:1-2). All those names! All those places! They mattered to Luke, who was quite a historian. These verses remind us that our faith is based on more than some general idea about God. We celebrate God the Creator entering into human history.

John's call to repent and to prepare the way of the Lord is for us, too— in our own time and place in God's story. Sometimes, we hear this reading from Luke during the frenzy of December at a time when we are caught up in Christmas shopping, either in busy stores or as we shop online. We buy more possessions for ourselves and others than we need or even want, hoping that material gifts will convey our love— even as we are vaguely aware of the unjust working conditions of many who produce, pack and ship our gifts for us. Many of the same people who work in retail are the very ones who can't afford to put food on their own tables or pay their rent.

We also live in a time and place where it is easy for people to push faith to the side. Yet even when we are distracted by other things, we often realize, deep down, that we are missing something big.

St. Augustine is often quoted as saying, "O God, our hearts are restless until they rest in thee."

John's call to repent is just what we need to turn us around, and so we pray, in the words of the hymn:

"Confront us and heal us, until we all learn
the life that is ours when we're willing to turn."

—What do you need to turn from?
—What do you need to turn toward?
—What turning do we need to do as a church? A community? A nation?

Read Luke 3:7-18, including these words:

7 John said to the crowds that came out to be baptized by him, "You brood of vipers! Who warned you to flee from the wrath to come? 8 Bear fruits worthy of repentance. Do not begin to say to yourselves, 'We have Abraham as our ancestor'; for I tell you, God is able from these stones to raise up children to Abraham. 9 Even now the ax is lying at the root of the trees; every tree therefore that does not bear good fruit is cut down and thrown into the fire."

10 And the crowds asked him, "What then should we do?" 11 In reply he said to them, "Whoever has two coats must share with anyone who has none; and whoever has food must do likewise…" (Luke 3:7-11)

If I Have Two Coats

LYONS 10.10.11.11 ("O Worship the King,
All Glorious Above!")

If I have two coats, God calls me to share;
There's someone nearby with no coat to wear.
And if I don't know who that person might be,
It's to a new friendship that God's calling me.

If I have some bread — and soup, all the more —
I'm called to reach out to someone who's poor.
And if I don't know who that person might be,
It's to a new table that God's calling me.

If money is mine, God calls me to live
As someone who loves to generously give;
And if I don't know someone suffering near me,
It's to a new neighbor that God's calling me.

O God of great truth, John's call to obey
Prepared us for Christ, who shows us your Way.
May we have the courage to try something new,
To reach to new neighbors and so welcome you.

Biblical Reference: Luke 3:7-18
Tune: Joseph Martin Kraus, 1784
Text: Copyright © 2015 by Carolyn Winfrey Gillette.
All rights reserved.
Email: carolynshymns@gmail.com
New Hymns: www.carolynshymns.com

Reflection - If I Have Two Coats

What a way to start a sermon: "You brood of vipers!" That's not how they taught us, in preaching class at Princeton Seminary, to draw in our listeners. John's message began with strong words and with a warning. Yet as people responded by asking questions about what they should do, John changed his approach. He started giving them practical instructions for living in obedience to God. John said, "Whoever has two coats must share with anyone who has none; and whoever has food must do likewise." (Luke 3:11).

John calls us to *account* for our lives. He also calls us to simply *count* the possessions *in* our lives. How many coats are in your closet? How many shirts and pairs of pants do you own? How many suitcases or duffel bags do you fill when you go on vacation?

Sometimes our possessions help us to care for ourselves and others. Sometimes they just get in the way. Years ago, Bruce and I went on a family vacation with our three small children. We flew out to Ghost Ranch, a Presbyterian Conference Center in New Mexico. We had a wonderful week! Yet we took too much stuff. We were weighed down by our possessions. We had to keep track of quite a few bags and suitcases in the airport, we had to squeeze everything and everyone into a rental car, and we eventually had to carry all those possessions up from the conference center parking lot to the lodging where we were staying on top of the hill at Ghost Ranch. What we owned got in the way of what we were trying to do.

John the Baptist calls us to give things away— not just because of our own need to downsize, but to help others and to build a more just and fair world. We know that people who are poor don't need our leftover junk; people need love and justice.

Yet there are ways we can responsibly move some of our possessions along to help create communities that re-use and recycle. We can join "buy nothing" groups in our communities. We can pass along books to others who might enjoy them. Once we lower the number of our possessions, we can enjoy living in smaller, less expensive, more energy-efficient homes. Instead of buying more things, we can use resources to help our neighbors.

The good news is that, in doing so, we also create new friendships, longer and wider tables of hospitality, and an awareness of our neighbors around us.

—What do you need the courage to do, as you seek to simplify your life and share some of your possessions?
—How can you make your table more welcoming?
—Where do you see Jesus in the people around you?
—When did someone give you a coat— or a car, a book, or a meal— when you particularly needed it?

Read Luke 3:21-22:

21 Now when all the people were baptized, and when Jesus also had been baptized and was praying, the heaven was opened, 22 and the Holy Spirit descended upon him in bodily form like a dove. And a voice came from heaven, "You are my Son, the Beloved; with you I am well pleased."

John Was Preaching in the Desert

NETTLETON 8.7.8.7 D ("Come, Thou Fount of
Every Blessing")

John was preaching in the desert,
calling people to repent.
When they heard his word of judgment,
many wondered what it meant.
John said, "Someone who is greater
comes with fire and Spirit, too.
See! I baptize you with water;
he will make your whole life new."

Jesus went down to the Jordan —
to be baptized on that day.
All at once, the heavens opened
as he paused to humbly pray.
Then a voice came down from heaven —
with the Spirit, like a dove.
At those waters, God affirmed him —
God's beloved, sent to love.

On this day when we remember
how our Savior was baptized,
God, we pause and pray and wonder
at the ways you change our lives.
As your Son went through the waters,
We rejoice! We're baptized, too.
We are called your sons and daughters;
may we go out serving you.

Biblical References: Luke 3:15-17; Luke 3:21-22
Tune: John Wyeth's *Repository of Sacred Music*, 1813
Text: Copyright © 2019 by Carolyn Winfrey Gillette.
All rights reserved.
Email: carolynshymns@gmail.com
New Hymns: www.carolynshymns.com

Reflection - John Was Preaching in the Desert

One of the things that impresses me about John the Baptist is that his sense of urgency was combined with a sense of humility. He knew the world needed to turn around in order to be ready for a Savior— yet he knew that he was not the Savior the world was waiting for.

Jesus, too, had a sense of humility. He came to bring us the Good News of God's reign, and he lived with a spirit of service and love for others. He chose to go down into the water to be baptized. And he prayed! He had a good conversation with God at that time when his ministry was about to begin. When the Spirit descended on Jesus, a voice also came from heaven, "You are my Son, the Beloved; with you I am well pleased" (Luke 3:22).

We live in a world where so many people are pushing to get ahead of others— in grocery store lines, in traffic, in measures of success in business, in the size of their houses and the number of their possessions. Many of us live in a culture where people are often identified by what they do for a living. So, we struggle to prove we are the best, the strongest, the most important. It is a joy to see the humility of both John and Jesus, and it is a grace-filled moment when we learn that we, too, are beloved by God, simply because we are God's children. This sense of being "beloved" is where our humble service begins.

—Do you have a sense of being "beloved" by God?
—What is the story of your baptism?
—When have you seen someone living the Christian life in a real spirit of humility?

Chapter 4

Read Luke 4:1-13, including these words:

1 Jesus, full of the Holy Spirit, returned from the Jordan and was led by the Spirit in the wilderness, 2 where for forty days he was tempted by the devil. He ate nothing at all during those days, and when they were over, he was famished. 3 The devil said to him, "If you are the Son of God, command this stone to become a loaf of bread." 4 Jesus answered him, "It is written, 'One does not live by bread alone.'" (Luke 4:1-4)

God, We Long for Our Own Comfort

HOLY MANNA 8.7.8.7 D ("God, Who Stretched the Spangled Heavens")

God, we long for our own comfort;
we want life that's full and sure —
Stones to bread, right now, abundant;
we forget what shall endure.
When we look to things around us
for our pleasure, out of greed,
God, we pray that you'll remind us:
it's your Word we really need.

We confess we push the limits;
faith gives way to testing pride:
"Be dramatic, make a statement,
prove that God is on your side."
When we're tempted to show others
that you'll do what we request,
God, remind us to be humble —
not to put you to the test.

We bow down to what is evil
to achieve the things we choose;
We don't see when sin is subtle;
we don't see what we might lose.
May we look again to Jesus
who, though tempted, turned from wrong.
By your Spirit, guide and lead us;
keep us watchful, faithful, strong.

Biblical References: Matthew 4:1-11; Luke 4:1-13
Tune: William Moore's *Columbian Harmony*, 1825
Text: Copyright © 2017 by Carolyn Winfrey Gillette.
All rights reserved.
Email: carolynshymns@gmail.com
New Hymns: www.carolynshymns.com

Reflection - God, We Long for Our Own Comfort

This hymn tells the story of Jesus' temptation in the wilderness. Matthew and Luke both tell the story of three specific temptations that Jesus faced; each of these gospel writers simply presents the actual temptations in a slightly different order.

We may be quick to overlook the temptations of Jesus because we can't relate to them specifically. Personally, I've never been tempted to turn stones into bread, to accept all the lands of the world as a gift, or to jump off a church tower. Still, we tend to think we can take the easy way rather than the more difficult way in faith or in life.

—When have you faced the temptation to seek your own comfort more than to be faithful?
—When have you said, "The ends justify the means," and when have you been willing to compromise your values and beliefs, possibly even hurting other people along the way, to get what you wanted?
—When have you thought you'd dip your toe into the water of danger, just because you could, just because you figured "you were on a mission from God" and surely God would keep you safe? For example, have people in your church ever said they didn't need a child protection policy because "this is a church!" and "surely everyone here will behave themselves"?
—When, in the words of the hymn, have you faced temptations that were "subtle"— so subtle that you didn't even recognize them as temptations to sin?
—What have you learned from the times you gave into temptation?
—What have you learned from the times you resisted doing wrong?
—Is it harder on you, personally, to give in to temptation or to resist it?

Read Luke 4:16-19:

16 When he came to Nazareth, where he had been brought up, he went to the synagogue on the sabbath day, as was his custom. He stood up to read, 17 and the scroll of the prophet Isaiah was given to him. He unrolled the scroll and found the place where it was written:

18 "The Spirit of the Lord is upon me,
    because he has anointed me
        to bring good news to the poor.
He has sent me to proclaim release to the captives
    and recovery of sight to the blind,
        to let the oppressed go free,

19 to proclaim the year of the Lord's favor."

Sing Out! Sound the Trumpets! Proclaim Jubilee!
TO GOD BE THE GLORY 11.11.11.11 with Refrain

Sing out! Sound the trumpets! Proclaim jubilee!
Through words from Isaiah, we came to be free;
For blest by the Spirit, Christ read from that scroll,
Proclaiming his mission: To make our lives whole.

Refrain:
>　　Hear the word! Sing it out! It's good news to the poor!
>　　Christ has come! Let us shout! We are captive no
>　　　　more!
>　　Lost sight is restored, and God's world is set free:
>　　Christ came to our world to proclaim jubilee.

But still, women struggle for lives free and fair,
And children are hungry, and loved ones despair.
Still, those long-oppressed or in prisons of fear
Are longing to call this their jubilee year.

Refrain

O God, through your Christ you knelt down to the earth,
And by your own Spirit, you give us new birth.
May we as your church have a passion to share
Your jubilee love with the world everywhere.

Refrain

Biblical References: Psalm 146; Luke 4
Tune: William Howard Doane, 1875
Text: Copyright © 1998 by Carolyn Winfrey Gillette. All rights reserved.
Copied from *Gifts of Love: New Hymns for Today's Worship* by
Carolyn Winfrey Gillette (Geneva Press, 2000).
Email: carolynshymns@gmail.com
New Hymns: www.carolynshymns.com

Reflection -
Sing Out, Sound the Trumpets! Proclaim Jubilee

In 1998, I submitted this hymn to a hymn contest by the PC(USA)'s national Presbyterian Women's organization. The Presbyterian Women decided to include this hymn as one of the many songs to be used at their national gathering. Later in the summer, the American Baptists also asked to use the hymn at their national gathering. A couple of years after that, I included this hymn as one of the 45 new hymns in my first book: *Gifts of Love: New Hymns for Today's Worship* (Geneva Press).

By the time I wrote this hymn, I had been serving as a pastor for twelve years. I had met with women who were being abused by partners and spouses. I had listened to parents weep and ask me how they were going to feed their children. I had worked with people who were trying so hard to piece their lives together, only to be knocked down again and again by structures and situations they couldn't control. I had seen how so many people were controlled by fear that led to hate-filled behavior.

What is the promise of a jubilee year? It's a promise of freedom from injustice and hunger and fear. It's a promise that we can start over.

Across our country and around the world, groups of Christians are working to free people who remain in jail due to unjust bail practices. At the Presbyterian Church (USA)'s General Assembly in St. Louis in 2018, an offering was received at the opening worship service of over $47,000. Church leaders and advocacy groups marched down the street to the County Justice Center. They bailed out quite a few people who were in jail for misdemeanors — people who were remaining in jail simply because they couldn't pay the cash bail required to get them out.

Across our country and around the world, God's people are working to free immigrants and refugees who are struggling to survive in camps at the borders of nations, including the United States. Other are working to free people who have been abused— helping them to see their own self-worth and to find the resources to rebuild their lives in safety. We are grateful for the work of a friend who is an immigration attorney; she has worked countless hours helping people who have been trafficked to find justice and begin new lives.

Here in Luke, and in this hymn, we sing the promise that Jesus cares about our real needs and concerns in this life. "For God so loved the world..." that God wants to give us salvation and wholeness in our families, communities and nation here and now— not just in heaven at some future time.

—What difference does it make that Jesus' first sermon was about his calling to care for people who were hurting and oppressed?
—What do you know about human trafficking in your county or region?
—When people are released from jail in your community, who helps them start over?

Read Luke 4:21-30:

21 Then he began to say to them, "Today this scripture has been fulfilled in your hearing." 22 All spoke well of him and were amazed at the gracious words that came from his mouth. They said, "Is not this Joseph's son?" 23 He said to them, "Doubtless you will quote to me this proverb, 'Doctor, cure yourself!' And you will say, 'Do here also in your hometown the things that we have heard you did at Capernaum.'" 24 And he said, "Truly I tell you, no prophet is accepted in the prophet's hometown. 25 But the truth is, there were many widows in Israel in the time of Elijah, when the heaven was shut up three years and six months, and there was a severe famine over all the land; 26 yet Elijah was sent to none of them except to a widow at Zarephath in Sidon. 27 There were also many lepers in Israel in the time of the prophet Elisha, and none of them was cleansed except Naaman the Syrian." 28 When they heard this, all in the synagogue were filled with rage. 29 They got up, drove him out of the town, and led him to the brow of the hill on which their town was built, so that they might hurl him off the cliff. 30 But he passed through the midst of them and went on his way.

They Raged At Jesus' Sermon
LLANGLOFFAN 7.6.7.6 D ("Lead On, O King Eternal")

They raged at Jesus' sermon
in Jesus' own hometown,
For in the things he taught them,
he turned life upside down;
It wasn't just their neighbors
who knew God's love and grace;
For Jesus said God favors
the ones we don't embrace.

God saved a foreign widow
and rescued her from drought,
For when she helped Elijah,
God also helped her out.
In Naaman, God's own favor
to others was revealed;
Though many locals suffered,
that Syrian was healed.

In this world's noise and clatter,
too often values shift;
We say Christ's words don't matter
and throw them off a cliff.
We push aside the stranger,
we walk right by the poor,
We disregard the prisoner
and say we matter more.

O God, your love is wider
than we can comprehend;
You reach to the outsider
and call the stranger "friend."
In Christ you gave a message
transcending time and place
May we your church have courage
to share your love and grace.

Biblical References: Luke 4:21-30; 1 Kings 17; 2 Kings 5:1-14
Tune: Traditional Welsh melody, from Daniel Evans' *Hymnau a Thonau*
(*Hymns and Tunes*), 1865
Email: carolynshymns@gmail.com
New Hymns: www.carolynshymns.com

Reflection - They Raged At Jesus' Sermon

Did you ever go back to the town you grew up in and try to take on a different role there? Did you go back to a school where you were once a student— to be a teacher? Did you go back to the church where you were baptized to give a sermon or make a presentation?

I heard a story from one pastor who went back to speak at a church his family had attended; after delivering what he thought was a really good sermon, he was shaking hands with people at the back of the sanctuary as they exited. Many people were complimenting him on what a fine sermon he had preached. Then one older woman came through the hand-shaking line and said, "Yes, I remember you! I was a friend of your parents, and I used to babysit for you and change your diapers!"

Have you gone back to family reunions and gatherings and found yourself pulled into the same squabbles you got into years earlier, when your siblings and parents were a growing family? Part of the challenge is that our home-town friends and families may expect us to be the same as we were before. What happened when a hometown carpenter went back home as a preacher, a teacher— as the Savior of the World?

In that moment, when Jesus' old friends and neighbors were questioning who he was, Jesus said, "No prophet is accepted in the prophet's hometown" (Luke 4:24). Then he used the opportunity to tell his listeners about outsiders who were welcomed, heard, and accepted by God. This angered many people who wanted to be reassured that they, and their own friends and neighbors, had the inside track to God's love.

—When have you found that you had changed— but others continued to treat you in the old ways?

—When has it been hard for you to take someone else's message seriously because of your old ways of thinking about that person?

—How have you seen God reaching wider, and welcoming the outsider?

—Who is on the outside, looking in, in your world? Who is God calling you to welcome, accept and listen to, today?

Read Luke 4:38-40:

38 After leaving the synagogue he entered Simon's house. Now Simon's mother-in-law was suffering from a high fever, and they asked him about her. 39 Then he stood over her and rebuked the fever, and it left her. Immediately she got up and began to serve them.

40 As the sun was setting, all those who had any who were sick with various kinds of diseases brought them to him; and he laid his hands on each of them and cured them.

As Simon Was Casting His Net in the Water
ASH GROVE 6.6.11.6.6.11 D ("Let All Things Now Living")

As Simon was casting his net in the water,
you called him to leave there the life that he knew.
He changed his priorities, went with his brother,
and started a new life of following you.
Yet when he rose up and left fishing behind him,
he still had a home and a mother-in-law;
Our family relationships that we have woven
are part of our life, Lord, and part of your call.

O Lord, as you went to that house to bring healing,
You showed us the heart of God's purpose and plan.
With love and with care, you brought health — so
    revealing
That lives are made whole by God's word and command.
In that present moment, you showed us God's future,
Where love is much greater than things that destroy.
May all homes be places where families can treasure
Your gifts of community, healing and joy.

In healing a woman, you put aside boundaries —
For women were often forgotten, unseen.
You reached out to bless her and showed grace and mercy
To one who was sick and considered unclean.
O Lord, she was glad for acceptance and healing!
She rose up to serve when her health was restored.
May we make our homes to be places of welcome
As you have reached out with your welcome, O Lord.

Biblical References: Mark 1:16-20, 29-29; Matthew 4:18-22, 8:14-15;
Luke 5:1-1, 4:38-41, Tune: Traditional Welsh melody
Text: Copyright © 2018 by Carolyn Winfrey Gillette. All rights reserved.
Email: carolynshymns@gmail.com
New Hymns: www.carolynshymns.com

Reflection - As Simon Was Casting His Net on the Water:

When many of us think of Simon Peter, we remember the story of Simon and Andrew leaving their fishing to follow Jesus and join him in his ministry. "As Simon Was Casting His Net in the Water" celebrates that story and also includes the story of Jesus healing Simon's mother-in-law. Here we find themes of home, healing, welcome, and acceptance. It is a joy to imagine this story of Jesus going into a family's home and bringing healing and wholeness to someone there.

—What are the ways we need God's healing in our individual families?
—What does your imperfect yet beloved-by-God family look like?
—How has Jesus entered into your home?
—When Jesus has brought you healing, how have you then served him?

Sometimes individual family members need physical or emotional healing. Often, though, our family *structures* need healing.   Communities and nations need healing so they can better welcome and support families.

—When our society works to provide better child care and elder care for vulnerable people in families, how can these things be forms of healing?
—How have you seen Jesus' love and healing break boundaries between people— as Jesus broke boundaries by caring for a woman in need?
—What is your church doing to care for families that are hurting?

Chapter 5

Read Luke 5:1-11, including these words:

9 For [Simon Peter] and all who were with him were amazed at the catch of fish that they had taken; 10 and so also were James and John, sons of Zebedee, who were partners with Simon. Then Jesus said to Simon, "Do not be afraid; from now on you will be catching people." 11 When they had brought their boats to shore, they left everything and followed him. (Luke 5:9-11)

Sons of Thunder, James and John
ST. KEVIN 7.6.7.6 D ("Come Ye Faithful, Raise the Strain")

Sons of Thunder, James and John,
left their father fishing —
For they found that they were drawn
into Jesus' mission.
Christ had strength to calm the sea
and to bring great healing;
He taught with authority —
God's own way revealing.

As they heard the things he taught —
love of God and neighbor —
Those ambitious brothers thought
they would ask a favor.
So they said, "Give just one thing;
let our words here guide you:
Jesus, when you reign as king,
let us sit beside you."

"Can you drink the cup I drink?
Can you take the suffering?"
Jesus told them, "Stop and think!
This is what I'm offering.
Tyrants reign o'er other folk,
rising to high places.
You must bear a servant's yoke
 if you want true greatness."

Christ, we love the honored place
and the seat of glory.
Now, remind us, by your grace,
of the gospel story:
You gave up your life —it's true! —
with a love unswerving.
May all those who follow you
seek a life of serving.

Biblical References: Matthew 4:21-22; Matthew 20:20-28; Mark 1:9-20; Mark 10:35-45; Luke 5:1-11; Acts 12:1-5 Tune: Arthur S. Sullivan, 1872
Email: carolynshymns@gmail.com
New Hymns: www.carolynshymns.com

Reflection - Sons of Thunder, James and John

This hymn is mostly the story of a conversation (see Mark 10:35-45) that Jesus had with James and John who were quite ambitious; they wanted to claim the best places in Jesus' coming reign. "Sons of Thunder, James and John," begins with a reference to an earlier time, recorded in Luke, when the two brothers left their father Zebedee and the family fishing nets because they heard Jesus calling them to follow him.

Sometimes as we are journeying through life, we get distracted in our faith. We ask our Lord for unreasonable things. Sometimes we are not happy with the way that our lives are shaping up.

Yet think back to the beginning. Think back to the first time you were aware of being a child of God. Think back to the first time you were aware of who Jesus is. Try to remember the place where it all started. Was it at a baptismal font? In a town diner when you were sharing lunch and a deep conversation with a friend? In a Sunday School class? In a grandparent's home as you listened to your grandparent pray? For James and John, this call story is where their journey with Jesus began.

—Where, like James and John— and Simon Peter, too— did you first sense the call of Jesus to follow?
—How has your understanding of faith changed over the years since that time?

Jesus' teaching in Luke, as well as in the other gospels, invites us to a life of serving— and often, of suffering because of our faith.
—When did you learn about the "serving" part of following Jesus?

Try writing down a timeline of your Christian faith.

Draw a line from left to right on a piece of paper, then add points along the way for important faith moments. Mark the joys and the times of suffering that have happened in your life along the way.

—How has your faith changed, in response to these things you have experienced?
—What is important for you to remember about your early experiences of faith and how they have shaped your life?

Chapter 6

Read Luke 6:20-26:

20 Then he looked up at his disciples and said:
"Blessed are you who are poor,
   for yours is the kingdom of God.

21 Blessed are you who are hungry now,
   for you will be filled.
"Blessed are you who weep now,
   for you will laugh.

22 "Blessed are you when people hate you, and when they exclude you, revile you, and defame you on account of the Son of Man. 23 Rejoice in that day and leap for joy, for surely your reward is great in heaven; for that is what their ancestors did to the prophets.

24 "But woe to you who are rich,
   for you have received your consolation.

25 "Woe to you who are full now,
   for you will be hungry.
"Woe to you who are laughing now,
   for you will mourn and weep.

26 "Woe to you when all speak well of you, for that is what their ancestors did to the false prophets.

Blessed Are the Poor Among You
PROMISES 11.11.11.9 with Refrain ("Standing on the Promises")

Blessed are the poor among you, Jesus said.
Blessed are you hungry ones who long for bread.
Blessed are you mournful when your tears abound.
God is turning everything around.
Hear the good news!
God is giving you the kingdom and the laughter.
God will fill you...
And you will know the joy that overflows.

Blessed are you weary who are long oppressed,
All because you follow God in faithfulness.
Leap for joy, for God will give you life anew.
Long ago, the prophets struggled, too!
Hear the good news!
God is giving you the kingdom and the laughter.
God will fill you...
And you will know the joy that overflows.

Woe to all you rich who live with blinders on,
Feasting at your tables till the food is gone.
Woe to you who laugh and live without a care,
Woe! when people praise you everywhere.
God has spoken:
You have all received your joy and consolation.
I was hungry...
But did you share what God had given you?

God, your way of working is a great surprise!
Help us all to see your world through faithful eyes.
Only in your kingdom is our true joy found.
By your Spirit, turn our lives around!
Yours is good news!
You have offered us the kingdom and the laughter.
Please, God, fill us,
And we will know the joy that overflows.

Biblical References: Luke 6:20-26; Matthew 25:31-46
Tune: Russell Kelso Carter, 1886
Text: Copyright © 1998 by Carolyn Winfrey Gillette. All rights reserved.
Copied from *Gifts of Love: New Hymns for Today's Worship* by
Carolyn Winfrey Gillette (Geneva Press, 2000).
Email: carolynshymns@gmail.com
New Hymns: www.carolynshymns.com

Reflection - Blessed are the Poor Among You

Many of us are more familiar with the "blessings" in
Matthew 5 than we are with the "blessings and woes" in
Luke 6:20-26. These woes, these warnings, from Jesus
remind us to pay attention to what is going on around us in
our communities. In the words of the hymn,

"Woe to all you rich who live with blinders on,
Feasting at your tables till the food is gone."
A friend once told me about a time when she and her
young daughter went to a chicken dinner restaurant.
They saw a man who was homeless sitting outside the
front door, off to the side. She tried to hurry her daughter
past him, so they could go in and order their food. Her
daughter said,"Mom, that man looks hungry! We could
get him a meal, couldn't we?"

Sometimes it is tempting to keep the blinders on. Then
there are the six-year-olds among us who have gone to
Sunday school and learned that Jesus wants us to stop
and help— and not to pass people by.

The hymn reminds us:

"God has spoken:
You have all received your joy and consolation.
I was hungry...
But did you share what God had given you?"

—What are the ways we choose to turn our awareness
away from people in need?
—What helps you to turn your attention back to the hurting
people Jesus calls us to love?

Read Luke 6:27-36:

27 "But I say to you that listen, Love your enemies, do good to those who hate you, 28 bless those who curse you, pray for those who abuse you. 29 If anyone strikes you on the cheek, offer the other also; and from anyone who takes away your coat do not withhold even your shirt. 30 Give to everyone who begs from you; and if anyone takes away your goods, do not ask for them again. 31 Do to others as you would have them do to you.

32 "If you love those who love you, what credit is that to you? For even sinners love those who love them. 33 If you do good to those who do good to you, what credit is that to you? For even sinners do the same. 34 If you lend to those from whom you hope to receive, what credit is that to you? Even sinners lend to sinners, to receive as much again. 35 But love your enemies, do good, and lend, expecting nothing in return. Your reward will be great, and you will be children of the Most High; for he is kind to the ungrateful and the wicked. 36 Be merciful, just as your Father is merciful."

Christ, Your Words of Love Confound Us
BEACH SPRING 8.7.8.7 D ("God Whose Giving
Knows No Ending")

Christ, your words of love confound us,
even as we give you praise,
for the lessons that you teach us
seem so far from this world's ways.
How can we love those who hate us?
How can we love enemies?
What of people who abuse us?
How can we love even these?

Make us mindful: love is action,
not a feeling that uplifts.
In each daily situation,
love's the greatest of all gifts.
It's the wiser, stronger person
who will break the chain of hate.
Love can usher in redemption;
love can make a people great.

Faced with those who seek to hurt us,
make us confident and free:
you don't call us to be helpless
but to stand with dignity.
Lord, when others are demanding,
may we know they matter more
than our money or possessions.
May we share, not keeping score.

If we love just those who love us,
where's the giving? Where's the grace?
Even sinners try to do this;
they have friends that they embrace.
May we do, Lord, unto others
as we'd have them also do.
You have shown us: Love is action!
May we love, and make things new.

Biblical References: Luke 6:27-38; Matthew 6:38-48; 1 Corinthians 13
Tune: *The Sacred Harp*, 1844; attributed to Benjamin Franklin White
Text: Copyright © 2019 by Carolyn Winfrey Gillette. All rights reserved.
Email: carolynshymns@gmail.com
New Hymns: www.carolynshymns.com

Reflection - Christ, Your Words of Love Confound Us

As I was writing this hymn, I was grateful to be able to read Martin Luther King, Jr.'s "Loving Your Enemies" sermon delivered at Dexter Avenue Baptist Church, November 17, 1957. The sermon is available online at The Martin Luther King, Jr. Research and Education Institute at Stanford University. I am grateful that *Sojourners* magazine has shared this hymn, along with several of my other ones, on their website.

Jesus' call to love our enemies is one of the most familiar yet challenging teachings of Jesus. Back in 2006, I was sitting in a hospital room with a dying patient and the patient's spouse. The room was quiet except for a wall-mounted TV that was giving us a steady stream of news from a 24-hour news show. All of a sudden we started to see and hear breaking news reports about a school shooting at an Amish school in Nickel Mines, PA, not too far from our community. A man had gone into the one room schoolhouse, lined up the girls, and shot a number of them. Later, we found out the shooter was also dead. There was so much sorrow and anger in that community and around the world because of that horrendous act of violence against children in their school.

Still later on, in our local community, we heard an additional detail about the story that amazed us. We heard that, on the same day as the shooting, some of the Amish families whose children had been shot had gone to the home of the shooter's wife and children, offering them gifts of food and forgiveness. The Amish community said, basically, that this was what it meant for them to be faithful. Offering love and forgiveness in the face of violence was the only way they could live as followers of Jesus. In the months that followed, people around the world heard the story of the Amish community's response, and many were amazed.

Some of us are "confounded" by Jesus' teachings about love and forgiveness. We don't know what to do with them. We believe that Jesus' words sound good in theory, but we struggle to live them out in practical ways. We wonder if we could have forgiven the shooter and embraced his family so quickly.

It is essential for people who are being abused to know that God is not calling them to remain in dangerous situations as victims of abuse. Forgiveness is not the same as continuing to be victims. People who are being oppressed certainly need to stand up for their rights and to know their value as beloved children of God— and the community needs to stand with them in their struggle for human rights. In the words of the hymn,

"Faced with those who seek to hurt us,
make us confident and free:
you don't call us to be helpless
but to stand with dignity."

There are ways to stand with dignity, to refuse to be victims, and at the same time to seek the good for others. Forgiveness frees the one who has been hurt as well as the one who has done the hurting. I am grateful for the witness of the Amish families from Nickel Mines who, in the midst of tragedy, made this so clear.

—How would your community be different if people followed Jesus' way of non-violence and used strength, intellect, wisdom, creativity, and resources to work for peace and fairness, instead of investing so much energy and resources in revenge?

Read Luke 6:29:

29 If anyone strikes you on the cheek, offer the other also;
and from anyone who takes away your coat do not
withhold even your shirt.

Read also Luke 22:49-51:

49 When those who were around him saw what was
coming, they asked, "Lord, should we strike with the
sword?" 50 Then one of them struck the slave of the high
priest and cut off his right ear. 51 But Jesus said, "No more
of this!" And he touched his ear and healed him.

You Turn Mourning into Dancing
HYMN TO JOY 8.7.8.7 D ("Joyful, Joyful, We Adore Thee")

You turn mourning into dancing,
you give peace in times of strife;
You turn weapons made for fighting
into tools that nurture life.
God of love, you give a vision
of a time when war will cease,
And you call us as your children
to embrace your way of peace.

Through the ages, some have answered,
seeking mercy more than might.
Some have struggled just to whisper,
"God does not want me to fight!"
Some have stood in opposition
to the ways that lead to war.
Some have made the firm decision:
Peace is worth our working for!

May we learn that peace and justice
mean much more than saying, "No!"
Peace requires our daily practice,
seeds of listening need to grow,
Justice can indeed be costly,
love can put us to the test,
And nonviolence must be nurtured —
yet in seeking peace, we're blessed!

May we journey with our neighbors
in the struggles they go through;
To accompany another
is a peace-filled thing to do.
May we change our laws and culture
that give guns priority;
May we care for earth and nature,
seeking to be fossil free.

When we're driven to distraction
at the hatred and the fear,
When we struggle to take action
as we grieve the violence here,
Turn our mourning into dancing!
May our songs of joy increase
As we see what you are doing
in our midst, O God of peace!

Biblical References: Psalm 30:11; Isaiah 2:4; Micah 6:8;
Matthew 5:9,6; Matthew 26:51-52; Luke 6:29;
Luke 22:49-51, Romans 15:33
Tune: Ludwig van Beethoven, 1824
Email: carolynshymns@gmail.com
New Hymns: www.carolynshymns.com

Reflection - You Turn Mourning into Dancing

I wrote this hymn for the 75th anniversary of the Presbyterian Peace Fellowship. It lifts up Jesus' call to non-violence. Note the second verse:

"Through the ages, some have answered,
seeking mercy more than might.
Some have struggled just to whisper,
'God does not want me to fight!'"

I wrote these words remembering my father, a pacifist who courageously refused to participate in war at a time when that was a particularly difficult choice. His unwillingness to fight put him in opposition to members of his community and even to members of his own family.

My father was not an activist. He simply knew that, because he was a Christian, he could not kill another human being. He had to defend that stance in front of authorities who tried to convince him he was being unpatriotic. He had to go against the wishes of loved ones who would have been proud to have him go to war. At one point, he gave up a career teaching college physics classes because that would have involved him in training people who might then help to make nuclear weapons. He got a job teaching college English classes instead. Sometimes he taught community college classes at the state prison near our home.

Later in his life, when he was my father and I was his young daughter, he talked to me about how he had had to resist a system that had pushed him toward violence when he had simply wanted to live a quiet life in peace. One night, after we had watched yet another Vietnam War body count on the evening news, my father said to me, "I am afraid that you will grow up in a world where you will have

to make difficult decisions— where you will have to stand against the crowd— and it won't be easy for you."
Through the years, I have thought about my place in the world and in the church, and how this has been true. So— while this hymn is for the Presbyterian Peace Fellowship, the second verse is in memory of my father. That verse continues:

"Some have stood in opposition
to the ways that lead to war.
Some have made the firm decision:
Peace is worth our working for!"

His witness taught me:
"Justice can indeed be costly,
love can put us to the test,
And nonviolence must be nurtured —
yet in seeking peace, we're blessed!"

—When have you had to stand uncomfortably against the crowd in order to say, "I will not participate in violence and injustice"?
—What are the ways you have worked within the system to counter violence and injustice?

Chapter 7

Read Luke 7:1-10:

1 After Jesus had finished all his sayings in the hearing of the people, he entered Capernaum. 2 A centurion there had a slave whom he valued highly, and who was ill and close to death. 3 When he heard about Jesus, he sent some Jewish elders to him, asking him to come and heal his slave. 4 When they came to Jesus, they appealed to him earnestly, saying, "He is worthy of having you do this for him, 5 for he loves our people, and it is he who built our synagogue for us." 6 And Jesus went with them, but when he was not far from the house, the centurion sent friends to say to him, "Lord, do not trouble yourself, for I am not worthy to have you come under my roof; 7 therefore I did not presume to come to you. But only speak the word, and let my servant be healed. 8 For I also am a man set under authority, with soldiers under me; and I say to one, 'Go,' and he goes, and to another, 'Come,' and he comes, and to my slave, 'Do this,' and the slave does it." 9 When Jesus heard this he was amazed at him, and turning to the crowd that followed him, he said, "I tell you, not even in Israel have I found such faith." 10 When those who had been sent returned to the house, they found the slave in good health.

A Roman Centurion Sought Out the Lord
ST. DENIO 11.11.11.11 ("Immortal, Invisible,
God Only Wise")

A Roman centurion sought out the Lord:
"My servant is suffering, but just give the word!
For I have authority; you have it, too.
I know he'll be well with a blessing from you."

Then Jesus responded to those who were near,
"There's not, in God's people, the faith I've found here.
And someday God's kingdom will bring a surprise
With outsiders in and the heirs left outside."

The Lord sent him home and it soon was revealed
That just at that moment, the servant was healed.
That outsider saw it; may we see it, too:
That Christ has the power to make our lives new.

Biblical References: Matthew 8:5-13; Luke 7:1-10
Tune: Traditional Welsh hymn, in John Robert's *Caniadau y Cyssegr*
(*Songs of the Sanctuary*), 1839
Text: Copyright © 2014 by Carolyn Winfrey Gillette. All rights reserved.
Email: carolynshymns@gmail.com
New Hymns: www.carolynshymns.com

Reflection - A Roman Centurion Sought Out the Lord

For our 30th wedding anniversary, Bruce and I spent a wonderful week in Northern Ireland. Our hosts were the parents of an exchange student who had once stayed in our home for a month. Our new friends offered us gracious hospitality, and they gave us a wonderful tour of Northern Ireland and the Republic of Ireland. During the course of the week, we learned more about "The Troubles" — the years of conflict that caused so much death and despair. Thankfully, when we were visiting there, things were getting better, and there were plenty of signs of reconciliation. People on both sides were enjoying living in relative peace. It was good for the families, the communities, and the economy. It was good for justice.

On the plane coming home, Bruce and I were reflecting on this biblical text about Jesus healing the Centurion's servant. We remembered a conversation with one of our Northern Irish hosts who said this healing story was one of his favorite stories in the Bible. We remembered that Jesus not only healed the slave physically; he also brought healing of a different kind by being willing to help a Centurion— an enemy, part of an occupying army.

In Northern Ireland, we saw how opposing factions were finally working for reconciliation. Long-time divisions were being mended. It was good to see the ways that Jesus' love was continuing to overcome the separation and brokenness that had divided people from each other for so long. In the words of the hymn,

"And someday God's kingdom will bring a surprise
With outsiders in and the heirs left outside."

Christ's reconciling love has the power to bring us together with new people in surprising ways; this, too, is a form of healing. —When have you been surprised by the people that Jesus welcomes in?

Read Luke 7:11-17; 22, 36-50, including these words:

11 Soon afterwards he went to a town called Nain, and his disciples and a large crowd went with him. 12 As he approached the gate of the town, a man who had died was being carried out. He was his mother's only son, and she was a widow; and with her was a large crowd from the town. 13 When the Lord saw her, he had compassion for her and said to her, "Do not weep." 14 Then he came forward and touched the bier, and the bearers stood still. And he said, "Young man, I say to you, rise!" 15 The dead man sat up and began to speak, and Jesus gave him to his mother…

22 And he answered them, "Go and tell John what you have seen and heard: the blind receive their sight, the lame walk, the lepers are cleansed, the deaf hear, the dead are raised, the poor have good news brought to them.

36 One of the Pharisees asked Jesus to eat with him, and he went into the Pharisee's house and took his place at the table. 37 And a woman in the city, who was a sinner, having learned that he was eating in the Pharisee's house, brought an alabaster jar of ointment. 38 She stood behind him at his feet, weeping, and began to bathe his feet with her tears and to dry them with her hair… (Luke 7:11-15, 22, 36-38)

O Christ, You Are Life

LYONS 10.10.11.11 ("O Worship the King,
All Glorious Above!")

O Christ, you are life! You heal and restore!
You bring God's good news to those lost and poor.
Through all of your ministry here on the earth,
You looked in the crowds and saw each person's worth.

You entered a town; a widow was there.
She grieved for her son and cried in despair.
On seeing her sorrow, you raised up her son;
The neighbors all shouted, "A prophet has come!"

You went to a house and sat down to eat;
A woman in tears anointed your feet.
Your host muttered, "Sinner!" but you turned to say,
"She's joyful because she's forgiven today!"

O God, give us life and show us anew:
Each person is loved and valued by you.
May we see all people as children of yours,
And work for your kingdom that heals and restores.

Biblical Reference: Luke 7:11-17, 36-50, 7:22, 15:1-32, 4:18
Tune: Joseph Martin Kraus, 1784; until recently attributed to Johann
Michael Haydn
Text: Copyright © 2010 by Carolyn Winfrey Gillette. All rights reserved.
Email: carolynshymns@gmail.com
New Hymns: www.carolynshymns.com

Reflection - O Christ, You Are Life

I wrote this hymn for Bread for the World's *Bread for the Preacher.* Luke's stories of Jesus raising the widow's son at Nain (Luke 7:11-17) and forgiving a sinful woman (Luke 7:36-50) tell us about how Jesus lives out his teachings of compassion for the poor and the outcast.

One joyful part of this story and many stories of Jesus is that Jesus really noticed the people who were around him — people who were often invisible to others. Some of the best leaders of organizations are the ones who take the time to get to know the people around them. They're the ones who can walk into the office and greet the receptionist, the custodian, the mail carrier, the housecleaning staff person, by name. They're the ones who ask the cafeteria staff, "How is your son doing? Is he still working up in Pittsburgh?… How are you? I know last week was the anniversary of your husband's death…" In the words of the hymn,

"Through all of your ministry here on the earth,
You looked in the crowds and saw each person's worth."

When we know people's names, we are more likely to learn their stories. When we learn their stories, we are more likely to advocate for a world that values them as children of God.

—Have you ever known someone who does this— who sees everyone's worth and knows everyone's name?
—Do you know the names of the people around you?
—Who are the people who do cleaning where you work or in your church?
—Who is the person who delivers your mail?
—Who are the people who care for your loved ones in a nursing home?

—What are the names of your immediate neighbors, and what are their immediate concerns and needs?

—Who are the people who deliver your groceries or work at the farm stand in the summer?

—Who is the young person who puts groceries on the shelf at your favorite store?

—Who are the children who sit with their grandparents in the pew behind you on Sunday?

Read Luke 7:31-35:

31 "To what then will I compare the people of this generation, and what are they like? 32 They are like children sitting in the marketplace and calling to one another,
'We played the flute for you, and you did not dance;
  we wailed, and you did not weep.'

33 For John the Baptist has come eating no bread and drinking no wine, and you say, 'He has a demon'; 34 the Son of Man has come eating and drinking, and you say, 'Look, a glutton and a drunkard, a friend of tax collectors and sinners!' 35 Nevertheless, wisdom is vindicated by all her children."

Who Is Like This Generation?
BEACH SPRING 8.7.8.7 D ("God Whose Giving Knows No Ending")

Who is like this generation
and to what do they compare?
They're like children who are saying,
"We've played songs and you don't care!
You won't join us in our dancing!
You won't join the games we bring!"
As we dwell on our own doing,
God, we miss the song you sing.

We have longed for wealth and greatness —
to be beautiful and strong.
We have turned our eye from justice,
but you would not go along.
We have moved with great ambition,
our position to enhance.
Then we've viewed you with suspicion
when you would not join our dance.

When we scorn what's good for others
till they hunger and they thirst,
When we hurt your sons and daughters,
when we put our comfort first,
When our songs are loud and hollow,
when pride rises up and roars,
Show us what it means to follow
when the pipe and dance are yours.

Christ, remind us what you taught us:
you said, "Blessed are the meek" —
And your dance proclaims forgiveness;
God's own love is what you speak!
May the song of love you've given
be the music that we hear;
Send us dancing for your kingdom
as we seek to serve you here.

Biblical References: Matthew 11:12-22; Luke 7:27-37; Matthew 5:5
Tune: *The Sacred Harp*, 1844; attributed to Benjamin Franklin White
Text: Copyright © 2017 by Carolyn Winfrey Gillette. All rights reserved.
Email: carolynshymns@gmail.com
New Hymns: www.carolynshymns.com

Reflection - Who Is Like This Generation?

"Who Is Like This Generation?" is a prayer that we as the church will align ourselves with the song and dance of God's reign by following Jesus' Way.

Sin is basically being out of alignment with God's way of love shown to us in Jesus Christ. We often complain to people when we disagree with them: "You don't understand me!" "You don't get it!" "You have it all wrong!" That usually means that our values and theirs are not the same.

Sometimes, we even tell Jesus he is wrong. We may not do it in those exact words, but we act like we know better than Jesus. We say in a Sunday school class or after a challenging sermon:

"Jesus said to love our enemies, but he didn't have to deal with the problems of *our* society."

"Jesus said to forgive, but he didn't know [insert name of your worst enemy here]."

"I can do whatever I want with my money… my time… my possessions."

"Maybe Jesus said to love our neighbors, but if I don't want to get vaccinated, that's my business! If I put other people at risk, that's *their* problem! They should just stay home!"

Most recently, we have heard some people advocating for nationalism, violence and revenge, saying: "We tried it Jesus' way, and it didn't work."

These kinds of things are all a way of saying we think we have a better idea about how to do things than Jesus does. In the words of the hymn,

"We have longed for wealth and greatness —
to be beautiful and strong.
We have turned our eye from justice,
but you would not go along.
We have moved with great ambition,
our position to enhance.
Then we've viewed you with suspicion,
when you would not join our dance."

It is not Jesus' job to join *our* dance. It is our calling to
follow Jesus.

—When have you complained that Jesus' way is not
practical in this world we live in?
—When have you realized that you were the one who was
out of step with Jesus?
—How does God call you to dance in step with Jesus, and
to listen to the music of love?

Chapter 8

Read Luke 8:4-8:

4 When a great crowd gathered and people from town after town came to him, he said in a parable: 5 "A sower went out to sow his seed; and as he sowed, some fell on the path and was trampled on, and the birds of the air ate it up. 6 Some fell on the rock; and as it grew up, it withered for lack of moisture. 7 Some fell among thorns, and the thorns grew with it and choked it. 8 Some fell into good soil, and when it grew, it produced a hundredfold." As he said this, he called out, "Let anyone with ears to hear listen!"

Once a Farmer Went Out Sowing

AR HYD Y NOS 8.4.8.4.8.8.8.4 ("All Through the Night")

"Once a farmer went out sowing,"
Jesus began.
"Soon the tender plants were growing
there on his land.
Every day he labored, tending,
weeding, working, hope unbending.
So his care was never-ending
for what he'd planned."

God of love, when he was sleeping,
his harvest grew.
Even with his faithful keeping,
life came from you.
You awakened seeds he'd sown there;
you gave strength to what was grown there.
He was never all alone there;
he looked to you.

Long ago our church was planted
here in this place.
Those who loved you worked and tended
in your embrace.
Here they built a place of worship,
labored well in faith and friendship,
Preached and served in times of hardship,
all by your grace.

In our joyful celebration,
God, this is true:
You sustain this congregation;
life comes from you.
In the times we pray and gather,
when we risk for things that matter,
as we love and serve our neighbor,
we trust in you.

Biblical References: Matthew 13:1-9; Mark 4:26-29; Luke 8:4
Tune: Traditional Welsh melody
Email: carolynshymns@gmail.com
New Hymns: www.carolynshymns.com

Reflection - Once a Farmer Went Out Sowing

I wrote this hymn for the anniversary of a small Presbyterian Church in Delaware. The image of a sower planting seeds is a powerful one. Planting gives hope as it lifts up all kinds of possibilities for the future. What will you grow? How big will the harvest be? At that wonderful church anniversary celebration, church members, presbytery staff, and friends sang this hymn with great joy, enthusiasm and hope.

It wasn't too many years before that particular congregation closed its doors. Their numbers had diminished. There were not enough volunteers to do the basic things that a church needed to do. There were challenges that could not be overcome easily. So the church stopped being a church. The few remaining members went elsewhere, to other congregations. The building was empty. The church sign out front stood blank. There was nothing for it to announce— no worship times, no Sunday school, no suppers or mission events. Where was the hope in that? Where was the harvest?

Then a new planting began. Bruce and I were serving a neighboring church in Delaware, and our congregation began hosting a Ghanaian immigrant fellowship in our church's building. Each Sunday morning, they met in our gym— the only room available at that time. Occasionally we met together, as one, but usually their sermons, prayers and singing were in Twi, and ours were in English, so we met in different rooms of the church. Bruce and I used to preach for the Ghanaian fellowship and serve communion once a month in their worship service in the gym. The singing was beautiful. Sometimes our church members enjoyed going to their covered dish suppers, and some-times they came to our parenting classes and movie nights. Together, we planted many seeds of love.

When the time was ripe for the harvest, it was in the form of a new planting— a church planting. This immigrant fellowship became the Olivet Presbyterian Church— a Presbyterian church worshiping in the Ghanaian way. Through the generosity, guidance and help of the presbytery, they were able to begin meeting in the church building that had become vacant and available for their use.

A few times, when we were on vacation, we went and worshiped with our friends at the new Ghanaian church. Once again we could sing to God and affirm the words of the hymn that had first been sung in that building:

"You sustain this congregation;
Life comes from you."

—How is God sowing seeds of love through your congregation?
—Have you ever experienced a time when the seeds seemed to die for a while?
—How and when has God's harvest been a surprising one to you?

Read Luke 8:16:

16 "No one after lighting a lamp hides it under a jar, or puts it under a bed, but puts it on a lampstand, so that those who enter may see the light."

Read also Luke 11:33:

33 "No one after lighting a lamp puts it in a cellar, but on the lamp stand so that those who enter may see the light."

Like Lamps on the Lamp Stand
ASH GROVE 6.6.11.6.6.11 D ("Let All Things Now Living")

Like lamps on the lamp stand, we're made to keep shining,
for everything hidden will soon shine out bright.
God gives us a message that's meant for our sharing;
we're made to keep shining so all see God's light.
God's light is the love and the joy of the party
that God is inviting us all to attend.
May we who are hungry and thirsty and weary
all know God in Christ — and the love God extends.

Biblical References: Luke 8:16; Luke 11:33
Tune: Traditional Welsh melody
Text: Copyright © 2019 by Carolyn Winfrey Gillette.
All rights reserved.
Email: carolynshymns@gmail.com
New Hymns: www.carolynshymns.com

Reflection - Like Lamps on the Lamp Stand

A few years ago, I put together a service of hymns, scripture readings and prayers: "Singing In the Reign: A Worship Service Celebrating Jesus' Parables and Teachings in the Gospel of Luke." This service includes many hymns I had already written and a few new ones, too. This worship service of parables is available on my web site: www.carolynshymns.com "Like Lamps on the Lamp Stand" is one of the newer hymns that I wrote for this service.

The service includes the following wonderful stories and teachings of Jesus: New Wine and Old Wineskins, The Two Foundations, Two Debtors, A Lamp on a Lampstand, The Parable of the Sower, The Good Samaritan, The Mustard Seed, The Rich Fool, Repent or Perish, The Barren Fig Tree, The Great Dinner, The Lost Sheep, The Lost Coin, The Lost Son, Leaven in the Bread, The Rich Man and Lazarus, The Pharisee and the Tax Collector Praying, A Friend at Midnight, The Persistent Widow, The Eye is the Lamp of the Body, About Salt, The Thief at Midnight and Don't Fear, Little Flock.

When Jesus wanted to describe the reign of God, he often used parables — stories about ordinary things that were part of regular people's lives. These stories told of something bigger. They told of God's love, God's intention for the world, and the ways in which God is working among us.

This particular hymn, "Like Lamps on a Lampstand," contains just one verse, and it includes these words about Jesus' welcome and inclusive love:

"God's light is the love and the joy of the party
that God is inviting us all to attend."

Imagine Christmas lights. Imagine twinkling lights, stretched around a patio, for a summer evening picnic with friends. Think about the light of a campfire. Remember the times when a flashlight guided you or welcomed you home.

—How is God calling you to be the light that invites someone else home, to a place of love and welcome and joy?

Reflection - Like Lamps on the Lamp Stand

A few years ago, I put together a service of hymns, scripture readings and prayers: "Singing In the Reign: A Worship Service Celebrating Jesus' Parables and Teachings in the Gospel of Luke." This service includes many hymns I had already written and a few new ones, too. This worship service of parables is available on my web site: www.carolynshymns.com "Like Lamps on the Lamp Stand" is one of the newer hymns that I wrote for this service.

The service includes the following wonderful stories and teachings of Jesus: New Wine and Old Wineskins, The Two Foundations, Two Debtors, A Lamp on a Lampstand, The Parable of the Sower, The Good Samaritan, The Mustard Seed, The Rich Fool, Repent or Perish, The Barren Fig Tree, The Great Dinner, The Lost Sheep, The Lost Coin, The Lost Son, Leaven in the Bread, The Rich Man and Lazarus, The Pharisee and the Tax Collector Praying, A Friend at Midnight, The Persistent Widow, The Eye is the Lamp of the Body, About Salt, The Thief at Midnight and Don't Fear, Little Flock.

When Jesus wanted to describe the reign of God, he often used parables — stories about ordinary things that were part of regular people's lives. These stories told of something bigger. They told of God's love, God's intention for the world, and the ways in which God is working among us.

This particular hymn, "Like Lamps on a Lampstand," contains just one verse, and it includes these words about Jesus' welcome and inclusive love:

"God's light is the love and the joy of the party
that God is inviting us all to attend."

Imagine Christmas lights. Imagine twinkling lights, stretched around a patio, for a summer evening picnic with friends. Think about the light of a campfire. Remember the times when a flashlight guided you or welcomed you home.

—How is God calling you to be the light that invites someone else home, to a place of love and welcome and joy?

Read Luke 8:22-25, including these words:

22 One day he got into a boat with his disciples, and he said to them, "Let us go across to the other side of the lake." So they put out, 23 and while they were sailing he fell asleep. A windstorm swept down on the lake, and the boat was filling with water, and they were in danger. 24 They went to him and woke him up, shouting, "Master, Master, we are perishing!" And he woke up and rebuked the wind and the raging waves; they ceased, and there was a calm… (Luke 8:22-24)

O Teacher, Don't You Care?
LEONI 6.6.8.4 ("The God of Abraham Praise")

"O Teacher, don't you care?"
the Lord's disciples cried.
"The waves are beating everywhere —
We'll surely die!"
They called to him in dread,
for mighty storms could kill.
Then Jesus spoke into the fury,
"Peace! Be still!"

Lord, still the storm winds blow,
and still we cry in fear:
We too are sinking, don't you know?
Lord, are you here?
We seek to live your way,
yet sorrows beat us down.
We feel alone and wonder:
Where can peace be found?

Your church, your little boat,
is struggling in the seas.
We question if we'll stay afloat
in times like these.
The world is raging round;
there's trouble everywhere.
When we are facing mighty storms,
Lord, hear our prayer.

What strength and love you've shown!
So calm your church's fear.
Remind us that we're not alone,
for you are here.
And though the waves are strong
and winds blow where they will,
Your peaceful presence in our lives
is greater still.

Biblical References: Matthew 8:23-26; Mark 4:35-41; Luke 8:22-25;
Romans 8:31-39
Tune: Traditional Hebrew melody
Email: carolynshymns@gmail.com
New Hymns: www.carolynshymns.com

Reflection - O Teacher, Don't You Care?

There have been many artistic portrayals of Jesus calming the storm at sea. One of the most famous ones is by Rembrandt. The painting is dark and shadowed, as many of Rembrandt's paintings are. Yet if you look closely, you can see what the disciples are doing. Most of them are looking around in fear— but one of them is looking directly at the viewer. His gaze draws us into the painting. We can imagine ourselves in the boat. The disciple seems to be asking, "What would you be doing? What would you be thinking, if you were here?"

In a dear friend's cabin by a lake, there is a sign on the wall: "Pray toward heaven and row toward shore!" Jesus promises to be with us when the storms are rough and when we're far out on the lake. At the same time, he calls us to live responsibly and to put some effort into the safety of the people in the boat/world. In this world that is filled with many crises— climate change, a pandemic, economic inequality, famine and political unrest, and war— we are all in the same boat. As Christians, we are grateful that Jesus is in the boat with us.

—How do we pray toward heaven— trusting in Jesus to save us?
—How do we row toward shore— taking responsibility to help others in the boat and to steer the boat faithfully and well, so all will be safe together?

Read Luke 8:26-39, including these words:

26 Then they arrived at the country of the Gerasenes, which is opposite Galilee. 27 As he stepped out on land, a man of the city who had demons met him. For a long time he had worn no clothes, and he did not live in a house but in the tombs. 28 When he saw Jesus, he fell down before him and shouted at the top of his voice, "What have you to do with me, Jesus, Son of the Most High God? I beg you, do not torment me"— 29 for Jesus had commanded the unclean spirit to come out of the man. (For many times it had seized him; he was kept under guard and bound with chains and shackles, but he would break the bonds and be driven by the demon into the wilds.) 30 Jesus then asked him, "What is your name?" He said, "Legion"; for many demons had entered him. 31 They begged him not to order them to go back into the abyss.

32 Now there on the hillside a large herd of swine was feeding; and the demons begged Jesus to let them enter these. So he gave them permission. 33 Then the demons came out of the man and entered the swine, and the herd rushed down the steep bank into the lake and was drowned… (Luke 8:26-33)

One Day as Jesus Traveled
LLANGLOFFAN 7.6.7.6 D ("Rejoice, Rejoice, Believers")

One day as Jesus traveled
to places wild, untold,
He met a man unraveled
by evil's awful hold.
The demons that possessed him
saw Christ and screamed in fear;
They knew, in their resisting,
their days were numbered here.

That man knew only suffering,
a life of grief and pain;
He could not yet imagine
that he'd be whole again.
The demons cried to Jesus,
"Just send us to those swine!"
When evil faces goodness,
it seeks a new design.

When goodness meets great evil,
when faith encounters sin,
The field is never level,
for God's great love will win.
Yet legions cry in anger
while clinging to their days;
They seek to trouble longer,
to harm in other ways.

When churches seek to practice
the faith with which we're blessed
By seeking love and justice
and helping the oppressed,
So often there is tension
that tears the heart and soul,
A struggle, a resisting
of all that makes us whole.

The demons cried to Jesus,
"Just send us to those swine!"
Yet soon those pigs stampeded
right down a steep incline.
For things that bring destruction
will one day fall away;
And God is surely bringing
a new and joyful day.

Biblical References: Mark 5:1-20; Luke 8:26-39; Matthew 8:28-34
Tune: Traditional Welsh melody, from Daniel Evans' *Hymnau a Thonau*
(*Hymns and Tunes*), 1865
Email: carolynshymns@gmail.com
New Hymns: www.carolynshymns.com

Reflection - One Day as Jesus Traveled

This hymn tells the story of Jesus healing the man with demons in Gerasene, sending the demons into swine that then ran off a cliff. This is an uncomfortable story on several different levels. Many of us are uneasy talking about demons; we would rather think in terms of modern illnesses that we can understand scientifically. Also, what about those pigs? We don't want to hear stories of animals suffering, even if we think we understand the cultural and biblical reasons behind this bit of Luke's gospel.

The story does remind us, though, about the reality of evil, suffering and illness in our world. These things destroy. Sometimes our problems make us uncomfortable; sometimes they seem to send us hurtling off into the unknown.

As I write this, we are in the midst of a pandemic that has killed over 900,000 people in the United States alone. This vast number includes individual people we have known and loved, some of whom did the best they could to care for themselves by getting fully vaccinated, including my mother who died from Covid last fall. Because of her compromised immune system, the illness was simply too much for her.

In this biblical story in Luke, we find the promise that Jesus has power over all that could destroy or harm. In the words of the hymn,

"For things that bring destruction
will one day fall away;
And God is surely bringing
a new and joyful day."

When I think about the pandemic, when I grieve the suffering so many have faced, when I grieve my mother's death, these two hymn lines become, for me, an affirmation of faith. Before her death, Mom spoke to us about her trust in God to be with her and to love her always. In some way I can't fully comprehend, she has now experienced healing. She is in our Father's house that has many rooms, where Jesus prepared a place for her. Death did not win. Love will always win.

__What are the things that have, at times, destroyed peace and hope for you?
__Who has comforted you with the promise that Jesus brings healing?

Read Luke 8:40-56, including these words:

42 …As he went, the crowds pressed in on him. 43 Now there was a woman who had been suffering from hemorrhages for twelve years; and though she had spent all she had on physicians, no one could cure her. 44 She came up behind him and touched the fringe of his clothes, and immediately her hemorrhage stopped. 45 Then Jesus asked, "Who touched me?" When all denied it, Peter said, "Master, the crowds surround you and press in on you." 46 But Jesus said, "Someone touched me; for I noticed that power had gone out from me." 47 When the woman saw that she could not remain hidden, she came trembling; and falling down before him, she declared in the presence of all the people why she had touched him, and how she had been immediately healed. 48 He said to her, "Daughter, your faith has made you well; go in peace…" (Luke 8:42-48)

She Suffered Twelve Long Years
LEONI 6.6.8.4 ("The God of Abraham Praise")

She'd suffered twelve long years!
She longed to be made whole.
The pain to body, mind and spirit
tore her soul.
She felt the weight of shame,
the lonely days of doubt.
Till one day she heard Jesus' name
and she reached out.

As Jesus walked along,
a crowd was gathering fast.
The people jostled close to him
as he walked past.
She would not call his name;
perhaps a touch would do.
She brushed against his clothing's hem
as he passed through.

As soon as she reached out,
she felt her body healed.
She knew the kingdom blessing
of God's love revealed.
And Jesus sensed it, too.
"Who touched me?" Jesus said.
The woman came and told the truth
with fear and dread.

Yet Jesus' words were kind:
"Now daughter, go in peace.
Your faith has made you well
and healed you from disease."
He sent her on her way,
her health and hope restored.
Her life was changed
from her encounter with the Lord.

We've suffered many years
from things that should not be;
We're ill in our own lives
and in society.
Lord Jesus, now we pray
that you will heal us, too.
Give us the faith to reach out,
fully trusting you.

Biblical References: Mark 5:21-43; Matthew 9:18-26; Luke 8:40-56
Tune: Traditional Hebrew melody
Email: carolynshymns@gmail.com
New Hymns: www.carolynshymns.com

Reflection - She Suffered Twelve Long Years

This hymn tells the story of Jesus healing a long-suffering woman. I first paid attention to this biblical text when I was working as a college student at a United Methodist mission in the mountains of Southeastern Kentucky, back in 1980. While i was there, our group of volunteers visited some house churches up in the mountain— up in the hills and the hollers. I remember a father and son playing banjos and singing a song they had written, with the title: "If I could but touch the hem of his garment…" It was a song from the perspective of the woman who reached out to Jesus in a crowd, grasping for healing.

This biblical account is the story of a woman who was long-suffering, literally. Chronic illnesses can be hard to bear. The physical pain is bad enough, but sometimes family and neighbors just don't understand. Or maybe they can see the pain, but don't know how to help. In some cultures and communities, there is shame attached to illness, and there is long-lasting shame attached to illnesses that go on and on.

The good news of Jesus is that he showed compassion to the woman, and he continues to reach out to the ones we too often forget. The other good news of the story is Jesus' power to heal. We cannot fully understand the miracle stories, but we can be awed by them, and we can affirm that God still works in amazing ways today. As a pastor, I have heard people tell me about serious illnesses that went away suddenly and dramatically. I have seen people recover from emotional scars and move on to a place of healing and peace. These are things we do not understand, but we can still say, "Thank you!"

—What illness or brokenness have you had to deal with for a long time?

—What does it mean to you that Jesus saw this long-suffering woman, paid attention to her, and healed her?
—How does healing come today?
—How have you seen the Great Physician working through physicians, nurses, therapists, technicians and scientists?

Chapter 9

Read Luke 9:7-9:

7 Now Herod the ruler heard about all that had taken place, and he was perplexed, because it was said by some that John had been raised from the dead, 8 by some that Elijah had appeared, and by others that one of the ancient prophets had arisen. 9 Herod said, "John I beheaded; but who is this about whom I hear such things?" And he tried to see him.

Read also: Luke 3:18-20:

18 So, with many other exhortations, he proclaimed the good news to the people. 19 But Herod the ruler, who had been rebuked by him because of Herodias, his brother's wife, and because of all the evil things that Herod had done, 20 added to them all by shutting up John in prison.

In Halls of Wealth and Power
LLANGLOFFAN 7.6.7.6 D ("Rejoice, Rejoice, Believers")

In halls of wealth and power
where shadowed deals are made,
The heartless ones devour;
the helpless are betrayed.
The ones who make decisions
seem confident and strong
Yet sometimes blur divisions
between the right and wrong.

When Herod chose to wander
from living as he should,
John preached with mighty thunder,
"Repent and do the good!"
Then power danced with anger;
revenge went dancing, too.
When they all join together,
what evil they will do!

O God of love and justice,
when we feel sure and strong,
May power never tempt us
to venture toward the wrong.
In all of our endeavors,
give wisdom, Lord, we pray,
That we may love our neighbors
and seek your kingdom way.

In halls of wealth and power,
in home and neighborhood,
May we reject the evil
and turn to what is good.
May justice dance with mercy
and service dance with grace;
May nations lift the lowly
till peace and love embrace.

Biblical References: Matthew 14:1-12; Mark 6:14-29; Luke 9:9
Tune: Traditional Welsh melody, from Daniel Evans' *Hymnau a Thonau*
(*Hymns and Tunes*), 1865
Email: carolynshymns@gmail.com
New Hymns: www.carolynshymns.com

Reflection - In Halls of Wealth and Power

This hymn remembers the killing of John the Baptist which Luke mentions in a couple of different places. Herod had an arrogance that often comes with having too much power. His was the same attitude that leads large corporations to continue polluting the earth because they know they can get away with it. It's the same perspective that says, "Might makes right." It's the same belief that leads some people in Congress and State Legislatures to try to limit voting rights for Black and Brown communities because these leaders fear that, if those communities were to vote, the powerful ones might be cast down from their thrones.

In this hymn, I used the image of the *dance* that is in the biblical story, and I asked the question: What kinds of things dance together and spin out of control, causing pain and harm and even death? When nationalism dances with apathy, we move into a society where some people oppress others and where most people are so caught up in their own lives they don't even notice the building of hatred and prejudice. When poverty and overwork join that same dance, we begin to understand why people don't focus on justice; they are simply trying to survive. When underfunding dances with lack of laws protecting children, we find deeply wounded little ones being tossed around in the foster care system for years. When narcissism dances with Covid, we build a nation where people don't even pretend to care for and protect their neighbors' health. When power dances with anger and revenge joins in the dance, too, we have the story of a vindictive family that kills John the Baptist, and in modern times. We also have a war of aggression going on, where missiles are being fired at schools and hospitals in Ukraine, and where civilians who are fleeing are being shot in the streets.

—When you look at our world today, where do you see halls of wealth and power?

—What is an example of how the "confident and strong" blur divisions between right and wrong?

—When have you seen power dancing with anger in a way that hurts other people— especially when revenge joins the dance?

—How can governments— community, state, and national — use power for good?

—How can we, as citizens— find ways to use our power and influence for the good of society?

—What can be done by ordinary people, on the local level, to make your community a better place?

Read Luke 9:18-27, including these words:

18 Once when Jesus was praying alone, with only the disciples near him, he asked them, "Who do the crowds say that I am?" 19 They answered, "John the Baptist; but others, Elijah; and still others, that one of the ancient prophets has arisen." 20 He said to them, "But who do you say that I am?" Peter answered, "The Messiah of God." 21 He sternly ordered and commanded them not to tell anyone, 22 saying, "The Son of Man must undergo great suffering, and be rejected by the elders, chief priests, and scribes, and be killed, and on the third day be raised."

23 Then he said to them all, "If any want to become my followers, let them deny themselves and take up their cross daily and follow me. 24 For those who want to save their life will lose it, and those who lose their life for my sake will save it… (Luke 9:18-24)

Jesus Asked One Day
SHOWALTER 10.9.10.9 with Refrain ("Leaning on the
Everlasting Arms")

Jesus asked one day, "What do others say?
Who do people tell you that I am?"
His disciples said, "John — back from the dead,
Or a prophet sent by God's own hand."

Refrain:
Lord and Savior, you are the One who bore the cross;
May we follow, serving you no matter what the cost.

He said, "Tell me, then, who you say I am."
Peter answered, "You are God's own Son."
Jesus said, "You Rock! You're the building block
That my church will be established on."
Refrain

Jesus told his friends, "See how love extends:
I must suffer, die and then be raised."
Peter disagreed: "That can never be.
God's Messiah will know glorious days!"
Refrain

Jesus said to him, "Get behind me, then.
Those who cling to life will surely die.
Come and follow me! I will make you free.
Seek God's kingdom and you'll find new life."
Refrain

Biblical References: Matthew 16:13-25; Mark 8:27-38; Luke 9:18-27
Tune: Anthony J. Showalter, 1887
Text: Copyright © 2014 by Carolyn Winfrey Gillette. All rights reserved.
Email: carolynshymns@gmail.com
New Hymns: www.carolynshymns.com

Reflection - Jesus Asked One Day

I grew up going to summer church camps and singing "I Have Decided to Follow Jesus." I grew up listening to Sunday School teachers tell us that following Jesus means being willing to make great sacrifices and to serve others with love. This hymn tells the story of Peter's declaration about Jesus, Jesus foretelling his death and resurrection, the cross, and self-denial.

We find ourselves called to take up our cross in surprising ways. When I was a child, I imagined working in great mission fields far away. Church camp counselors described "giving your life" as one big dramatic moment. Now, I realize that following Jesus' way of love is a daily calling. It means thinking of others' needs during a pandemic— being willing to get vaccinated and wear a mask out of love of neighbor. Following Jesus' sacrificial way means giving generously to charities and justice organizations that our family believes are important. It means welcoming refugees into our local communities, schools, neighborhoods, and workplaces. Following Jesus very often means doing the simplest faith-filled things, again and again and again.

—What are the names and words you use to describe Jesus?
—What are the seemingly ordinary ways that Jesus calls you to be faithful, by doing the same thing again and again, each and every day?

Read Luke 9:28-36:

28 Now about eight days after these sayings Jesus took with him Peter and John and James, and went up on the mountain to pray. 29 And while he was praying, the appearance of his face changed, and his clothes became dazzling white. 30 Suddenly they saw two men, Moses and Elijah, talking to him. 31 They appeared in glory and were speaking of his departure, which he was about to accomplish at Jerusalem. 32 Now Peter and his companions were weighed down with sleep; but since they had stayed awake, they saw his glory and the two men who stood with him. 33 Just as they were leaving him, Peter said to Jesus, "Master, it is good for us to be here; let us make three dwellings, one for you, one for Moses, and one for Elijah"—not knowing what he said. 34 While he was saying this, a cloud came and overshadowed them; and they were terrified as they entered the cloud. 35 Then from the cloud came a voice that said, "This is my Son, my Chosen; listen to him!" 36 When the voice had spoken, Jesus was found alone. And they kept silent and in those days told no one any of the things they had seen.

One Day Jesus Climbed a Mountain
W ZLOBIE LEZY 4.4.7.4.4.7.4.4.4.4.7 ("Infant Holy, Infant Lowly")

One day Jesus climbed a mountain
to a place of prayer and rest.
Peter, James and John went with him
to that lonely wilderness.
In a moment so amazing,
Jesus shone with brightness blazing,
wrapped in glory, heaven-blessed.

Words could not contain the wonder
of that most amazing sight.
Jesus' face was bright with splendor
and his clothes were dazzling white.
There appeared two others with him;
Moses and Elijah met him
on that lonely mountain height.

Jesus talked there with the prophet
and the bearer of the Law.
When his three disciples saw it,
they were filled with joy and awe.
Peter told him, "Let us stay here.
We can worship God and pray here."
Then a cloud came over all.

From that cloud a voice was saying,
"This is my beloved son."
And the voice said, "Listen to him!" —
to God's faithful chosen one.
While their plans were filled with glory,
Christ was living out the story
of his prayer, "Thy will be done."

Jesus took them down the mountain
to a world of pain and loss.
For he knew what lay before him;
he must journey to the cross.
In his serving, in his healing,
God was there, by grace revealing
wondrous love comes at a cost.

Biblical References: Matthew 17:1-13; Mark 9:2-13; Luke 9:28-36;
2 Peter 1:16-18
Tune: Polish melody
Email: carolynshymns@gmail.com
New Hymns: www.carolynshymns.com

Reflection - One Day Jesus Climbed a Mountain

There are a number of hymns about Jesus' transfiguration. I wanted to write one with an easy, singable tune. I chose the tune W ZLOBIE LEZY ("Infant Holy, Infant Lowly") because it climbs with the words. As we sing this hymn, and as the tune rises in steps, we can almost imagine Jesus climbing a mountain with his disciples.

Many of my hymns tell a story from the Bible. As pastors, Bruce and I are finding that plenty of people are coming into churches for the first time. They want to learn the basics about faith. They are asking important questions: "What is the Lord's Prayer and what does it mean? What are the basic stories of the Bible that are important for me to know?" Who was the Prodigal Son? Who was the Good Samaritan? What does this word "Transfiguration" mean? Often, I write hymns as a way of teaching the biblical stories.

The Transfiguration itself is amazing. The Gospel writers seemed to have trouble even putting into words this thing that had happened to Jesus. Luke described Jesus' clothes, his appearance, and the two great biblical figures, Moses and Elijah, who appeared with him.

One of the beautiful parts of this story is the voice that says, "This is my Son, my Beloved. Listen to him!"

Listen to what?
…to his teaching about loving God, loving neighbors, loving enemies
…to his teaching that God is accessible to us and God loves us dearly
…to his teaching that God's table is a welcome table
…to his willingness to forgive others
…to his invitation that welcomes in people who are poor

…to his love for the outsider
…to his call to be perfect in love
… and to his call to humbly serve.

Notice that that's what Jesus did next— he served. After he went down from the mountain, he continued his ministry of healing and compassion, and he journeyed to the cross.

—Did you ever had an experience of God's presence that was indescribable to you?
Did you try to tell anyone? Who did you tell?
—How have you experienced Jesus' presence at the bottom of the mountain, in the midst of human need?
What did you do?

Read Luke 9:43b-48:

43 While everyone was amazed at all that he was doing, he said to his disciples, 44 "Let these words sink into your ears: The Son of Man is going to be betrayed into human hands." 45 But they did not understand this saying; its meaning was concealed from them, so that they could not perceive it. And they were afraid to ask him about this saying.

46 An argument arose among them as to which one of them was the greatest. 47 But Jesus, aware of their inner thoughts, took a little child and put it by his side, 48 and said to them, "Whoever welcomes this child in my name welcomes me, and whoever welcomes me welcomes the one who sent me; for the least among all of you is the greatest."

Who is Greatest in the Kingdom?
NETTLETON 8.7.8.7 D ("Come, Thou Fount of Every Blessing")

"Who is greatest in the kingdom?
Who among us is the best?"
The disciples were debating:
"In God's reign, who will be blest?"
Jesus, had those twelve forgotten?
Faithful living has a cost —
And to journey where you'd lead them,
they would journey to the cross.

"Who is greatest in the kingdom?"
The disciples heard your call:
"If you want to be the first one,
 you must be the last of all."
Do not think that high position
is a thing that you deserve!
"If you want to be the first, then,
be the first to humbly serve."

"Who is greatest in the kingdom?
Who will take the throne and reign?"
Christ, you put a child among them,
and you told them once again:
"If you give a child a welcome,
then you also welcome me."
Faithful service, not ambition,
builds up God's community.

Biblical References: Mark 9:30-37; Matthew 17:22-23, 18:1-5;
Luke 9:43b-45, 9:46-48
Tune: John Wyeth's *Repository of Sacred Music*, 1813
Text: Copyright © 2018 by Carolyn Winfrey Gillette. All rights reserved.
Email: carolynshymns@gmail.com
New Hymns: www.carolynshymns.com

Reflection - Who is Greatest in the Kingdom?

Jesus was talking about his upcoming death, and all the disciples could talk about was which one of them was the greatest. We can picture them walking along the road, talking loudly as if they owned the place, bragging a bit to each other about their accomplishments, jostling each other and playfully punching each other's shoulders, saying things like, "Well, did you see what I did back there! I bet you can't top that!" Sometimes they were so full of themselves.

Sometimes we are so full of ourselves, too. Look how I ran that meeting! Look how I grew that church! Have you noticed what's on my resume? I'm feeling pretty good about this award I just received!

Jesus' message to his disciples was this: See this child? Go ahead, this is what it's all about! Welcome this child! And while you're at it, remember that those of you who are least, like this little child, are really the greatest of them all.

—How does your church welcome children?
—How does your church learn from children about God's reign?

Chapter 10

Read Luke 10:25-37, including these words:

25 Just then a lawyer stood up to test Jesus. "Teacher," he said, "what must I do to inherit eternal life?" 26 He said to him, "What is written in the law? What do you read there?" 27 He answered, "You shall love the Lord your God with all your heart, and with all your soul, and with all your strength, and with all your mind; and your neighbor as yourself." 28 And he said to him, "You have given the right answer; do this, and you will live." (Luke 10:25-28)

God, We Thank You For the Churches

NETTLETON 8.7.8.7 D ("Come, Thou Fount of Every Blessing")

God, we thank you for the churches
that are sanctuaries here —
that give safety, love and refuge
to the ones who live in fear.
For our neighbors, God, are suffering,
and they're yearning to be free;
we give thanks for all the places
that give hospitality.

Christ, we thank you for your welcome
that tears walls and borders down,
that gives hope to people fleeing,
that helps churches stand their ground.
For our neighbors, Lord, are asking,
and they're wondering what we'll do.
May our churches give them welcome,
and so find we welcome you.

By your Spirit give us courage;
by your Spirit, keep us strong.
May we focus on your mercy;
may we sing your justice song.
For our neighbors are your children,
so prepare us, God, to be
safe and welcome sanctuaries
in your New Community.

Biblical References: Psalm 101:1; Micah 6:8; Matthew 2:1-15;
Matthew 25:31-46; Luke 10:25-37; Ephesians 2:14; Hebrews 13:2;
1 John 3:1
Tune: John Wyeth's *Repository of Sacred Music*, 1813
Text: Copyright © 2018 by Carolyn Winfrey Gillette. All rights reserved.
Email: carolynshymns@gmail.com
New Hymns: www.carolynshymns.com

Reflection - God, We Thank You For the Churches

One day when we were living and serving a church in Philadelphia, we attended a vigil outside a church that was providing sanctuary for an undocumented woman and her children. They were allowing her to stay in their building, around the clock, because the immigration officials would not arrest her when she was seeking sanctuary in the church building. It gave her time and safety to pursue her immigration case.

We had an opportunity to go inside the church and talk to this mother. I tried to imagine: What would it be like to feel alone, helpless and in danger, when you were just trying to protect your children? What would it be like to fear for your safety if you were deported to your home country? What would it mean to you to have a church say, "We will welcome you… We will walk beside you… You can stay here, and we will do our best to make sure you are safe while you appeal your case"?

This hymn is a prayer of thanksgiving for churches that provide safety and hospitality for neighbors who are fleeing danger. It is a prayer that all churches may have courage to stand with these neighbors in need. In our churches, we often talk about the importance of loving our neighbors, as Jesus taught us to do. Different churches will do this in different ways. Not all will declare themselves to be sanctuary churches. Many, will choose to serve by reaching out in their communities to help people who are poor, children who are hungry, older neighbors who are lonely.

Our churches do many good things that we can celebrate. It's good for all of us to ask the question: How will my church provide a welcome?

—Are their times when our charity needs to move toward justice?

—Are there times when your congregation needs to challenge the systems that allow people to be hurt?

—Are there ways you need to advocate for neighbors' basic human rights?

—Is it comfortable or uncomfortable for you to realize that churches are helping people who are undocumented?

—Is it comfortable or uncomfortable for you to realize that young children in our schools, the neighbor down the street, and people who are in our towns and neighborhoods face deportation to places where they might be killed?

Read Luke 10:29-37:

29 But wanting to justify himself, he asked Jesus, "And who is my neighbor?" 30 Jesus replied, "A man was going down from Jerusalem to Jericho, and fell into the hands of robbers, who stripped him, beat him, and went away, leaving him half dead. 31 Now by chance a priest was going down that road; and when he saw him, he passed by on the other side. 32 So likewise a Levite, when he came to the place and saw him, passed by on the other side. 33 But a Samaritan while traveling came near him; and when he saw him, he was moved with pity. 34 He went to him and bandaged his wounds, having poured oil and wine on them. Then he put him on his own animal, brought him to an inn, and took care of him. 35 The next day he took out two denarii, gave them to the innkeeper, and said, 'Take care of him; and when I come back, I will repay you whatever more you spend.' 36 Which of these three, do you think, was a neighbor to the man who fell into the hands of the robbers?" 37 He said, "The one who showed him mercy." Jesus said to him, "Go and do likewise."

O God, You Give Us Neighbors
AURELIA 7.6.7.6 D ("The Church's One Foundation")

O God, you give us neighbors
for whom your love abounds.
They've come here seeking refuge;
they work here in our towns.
Their children go to school here;
they come to church and pray.
O Lord, we grieve when neighbors
are being sent away.

O God, you give us neighbors
in this world that divides.
We see them at the border;
they're struggling for their lives.
They're hurting by the roadside,
and by the river, too.
You call us to show mercy
to neighbors loved by you.

O God, you give us neighbors
and call us all to see
our common fears and longings,
our shared humanity.
You call us all to listen
to burdens they have known,
to hear the truth they tell us,
to see the love they've shown.

O God, you give us neighbors;
and now, what must we do?
This question asked of Jesus
is one we ask anew.
May we not make excuses
and choose to walk on by
these neighbors fleeing violence —
some sent back now to die.

God, may we work for justice
for those who live in fear;
may we show Christ's compassion,
and pray and persevere —
and by your Holy Spirit,
in all we do and say,
may we stand up for neighbors
now being sent away.

Biblical Texts: Luke 10:25-46; Leviticus 19:33-34; Leviticus 24:22;
Matthew 25:31-46
Tune: Samuel Sebastian Wesley, 1864
Text: Copyright © 2019 by Carolyn Winfrey Gillette.
All rights reserved.
Email: carolynshymns@gmail.com
New Hymns: www.carolynshymns.com

Reflection - O God, You Give Us Neighbors

This hymn is based on Jesus' call for us to love our neighbors. In answer to the question, "Who is my neighbor?", Jesus told the story of the Good Samaritan. "O God, You Give Us Neighbors" is another hymn that lifts up immigrants as some of the people that God calls us to love. I wrote it at a time when deportations were very much in the news.

When we call people "undocumented" or worse, we find it easy to group them all into a big category we think of as "the other." Yet, year by year, our country is becoming more diverse. When I visit my hometown— the rural, western Maryland town where I grew up, a town that I remember as being almost all white— I notice that it is beginning to reflect the diversity of the rest of the country. I thank God for the wonderful variety of God's children who are coming here from many different places.

—Are you and your family immigrants? Recent ones? The children or grandchildren of immigrants?
—Are there immigrant children in your local schools? Are there immigrants working at local businesses? What are their hopes, dreams and fears? Does your church serve them? Does your church serve with them?
—Are there people in your community who are worried about their immigration status?
—Have local businesses been raided and have some of your neighbors, whose children go to school with yours, been sent away?

In the words of the hymn, we see neighbors "at the roadside," like the Good Samaritan, and "at the river, too," like people desperately trying to cross the Rio Grande at our Southern border of the United States. Sometimes we see news photos of bodies along the shore— of people who did not make it across.

Many of us were moved by a particularly painful photo of a father and child dead on the shore— the father's arm around the child, trying in his last moments to protect the little one from harm.

—What are the basic things in life that all people long for? Food and safety and what else?
—What immigration bills are now before Congress, and how can you help to work for justice and welcome for your neighbors?

Read Luke 10:38-42:

38 Now as they went on their way, he entered a certain village, where a woman named Martha welcomed him into her home. 39 She had a sister named Mary, who sat at the Lord's feet and listened to what he was saying. 40 But Martha was distracted by her many tasks; so she came to him and asked, "Lord, do you not care that my sister has left me to do all the work by myself? Tell her then to help me." 41 But the Lord answered her, "Martha, Martha, you are worried and distracted by many things; 42 there is need of only one thing. Mary has chosen the better part, which will not be taken away from her."

Martha Labored in the Kitchen
NETTLETON 8.7.8.7 D ("Come, Thou Fount of
Every Blessing")

Martha labored in the kitchen;
there was much yet to be done!
There was cooking, cleaning, baking —
too much work for anyone.
For the Lord had come to visit;
Jesus sat there as her guest.
So much work! She longed to share it,
so the meal would be its best.

Mary sat and humbly listened
to their guest — her Friend and Lord.
She just thought of Jesus' teaching —
not the need for bread and board.
So when Martha came complaining,
seeking Mary's help that day.
Jesus turned to her explaining,
"Mary chose the better way."

God, we see in her distraction —
Martha lost sight of her goal;
In her grumbling and complaining,
she forgot food for the soul.
For there's always something pressing —
something urgent we must do,
Yet for us there's also blessing
in the time we spend with you.

Were there days when Mary labored,
helping others, serving well?
Were there times when Martha savored
stories Jesus loved to tell?
May we worship, pray and study;
may we serve you well today!
All are needed on the journey
as we travel Jesus' way.

Biblical Reference: Luke 10:38-42
Tune: John Wyeth's *Repository of Sacred Music*, 1813
Text: Copyright © 2016 by Carolyn Winfrey Gillette.
All rights reserved.
Email: carolynshymns@gmail.com
New Hymns: www.carolynshymns.com

Reflection - Martha Labored in the Kitchen

This hymn is based on two sisters' responses to Jesus visiting to their home. Many of us can find ourselves in this story. Some of us are like Mary and some of us are like Martha.

Of course, the church needs both. All kinds of people, with all kinds of visions for ministry and with different personalities, are welcome in the church. In the words of the hymn, we pray,

"For there's always something pressing —
something urgent we must do,
Yet for us there's also blessing
in the time we spend with you."

It is also good to remember that we tend to stereotype Mary and Martha based on this story. For another view, look at John 11, at the story of Jesus raising Lazarus from the dead, where Martha got into more of a theological conversation with Jesus. All of us may respond differently at different times in our lives.

—Are you someone who always needs to be working hard and accomplishing things? Your work is surely a gift to the church and to your community.
—What are the ways you need to slow down, to let your soul be fed? What is soul-feeding for you?

People who follow Jesus need to take the time to listen and to pray— and also to serve. I enjoyed the recent movie, *A Beautiful Day in the Neighborhood* (with Tom Hanks as Fred Rogers), about Presbyterian minister Fred Rogers and his TV show, *Mister Rogers' Neighborhood.* I recall a wonderful scene in the movie about Fred praying for others by name as he was swimming laps in a pool, and it reminded me of the stories that I heard from

Presbyterian ministers who knew Fred as a friend; he made it a regular daily practice to pray for friends, acquaintances, and strangers. He took the time to pray.

While we think of Fred Rogers' faith, we also think of his wonderful, loving service to countless children who watched his show. Several times, I have heard adults describing years of abuse they suffered as children. One woman talked about being sexually abused by a parent. After the abuse, she would go and hide in her room and turn on a little TV that was in her bedroom. She would listen to Mister Rogers' kind voice saying, "I like you just the way you are." "You are special." As an adult, looking back, she said that Mister Rogers' ministry to children, on the air, saved her in those moments. His loving service to children saved her life because he taught her she was valued. He was able to see people as valuable because his life was one of both faithful prayer and humble service.

—What are the ways you care for yourself and others, perhaps offering hospitality and acceptance and love?
—What are the ways you feed your soul?

Chapter 11

Read Luke 11:1-4, 9-13, including these words:

1 He was praying in a certain place, and after he had finished, one of his disciples said to him, "Lord, teach us to pray, as John taught his disciples." 2 He said to them, "When you pray, say:
Father, hallowed be your name.
   Your kingdom come.   (Luke 11:1-2)

When Jesus Called You "Father"

AURELIA 7.6.7.6 D ("The Church's One Foundation")

When Jesus called you "Father"
in teaching folks to pray,
And when he said we're children
who need to trust your way,
O God, he knew your closeness,
your guidance from above.
Perhaps in Joseph's caring,
he'd learned to trust your love.

Some cannot call you Father;
they will not use that name.
The fathers they have known here
have caused them fear and pain;
And though you're like a father,
you're like a mother, too.
No single name can ever
tell all we know of you.

Yet Jesus in his teaching
described a father's joy
When, at his son's returning,
he ran to greet the boy.
O God, when we have hurt you
and struggled on our own,
Just like that loving parent,
you run to bring us home.

O God, you seek to save us,
no matter what the cost;
Our Father, your intention
is no one will be lost.
As Jesus called you "Abba,"
and trusted in your plans,
We trust in you to guide us!
Our lives are in your hands.

You hold your children's future
when all will be made new.
Your house has many dwellings
so we may live with you.
Just like a loving father,
you answer when we pray.
In thanks, may we your children
now follow you each day.

Biblical References: Matthew 6:9; Hosea 11:3-4; Deuteronomy 32:18;
Isaiah 66:13; Isaiah 49:15; Luke 15:11-32; Matthew 18:14; Mark 14:36;
Matthew 24:36; John 14:2-4; Luke 11:13;
Tune: Samuel Sebastian Wesley, 1864
Email: carolynshymns@gmail.com
New Hymns: www.carolynshymns.com

Reflection - When Jesus Called You "Father"

"When Jesus Called You 'Father'" is a new hymn celebrating the biblical references to God as Father. There are many positive images of Father, both in the Bible and in our world. Fathers can be strong, guiding influences in children's lives, they can be protectors, they can be nurturing, and they can be forgiving. "Father" is one of many images we can use for God.

This hymn is a reminder that no one name or title can give justice to the One who is beyond our human comprehension. Further, while the name, "Father," brings great comfort to some people, what does it mean to people who were abused by a father? What does it mean to a child who experienced disapproval from a father— to a child who was sent away with the hateful words, "Don't come back!"

The Bible is filled with names for God. The Bible is filled with names for Jesus. Sometimes, God is described as an eagle caring for her young (Deuteronomy 32:11) or as a mother who will not forsake her nursing child. (Isaiah 49:15). Jesus compares himself to a mother hen taking care of her chicks (Luke 13:34). Jesus tells three lost and found parables, comparing God to a shepherd seeking a lost sheep, a woman seeking a lost coin, and a father who runs to welcome his lost son home. (Luke 15).

—What words and images help you understand who God is?

Chapter 12

Read Luke 12:32-48, including these words:

32 "Do not be afraid, little flock, for it is your Father's good pleasure to give you the kingdom. 33 Sell your possessions, and give alms. Make purses for yourselves that do not wear out, an unfailing treasure in heaven, where no thief comes near and no moth destroys. 34 For where your treasure is, there your heart will be also. 35 "Be dressed for action and have your lamps lit… (Luke 12:32-35)

Don't Fear, Little Flock

ASH GROVE 6.6.11.6.6.11 D ("Let All Things Now Living")

"Don't fear, little flock!" Jesus lovingly told us,
"For it is your Father's good pleasure to give."
While fear, greed and hatred might seem now to hold us,
God offers a kingdom — a new way to live.
So sell your possessions, give gifts to the needy,
Make purses that nothing on earth can destroy.
God's treasure can never be bought by the greedy;
It's made out of justice, compassion and joy.

Don't fear, little flock, don't be filled with distraction,
When powerful people cause suffering and hurt.
Light lamps for God's kingdom, be ready for action,
Seek new ways of serving; O Church, stay alert!
Show kindness to all and show love to your neighbor,
Help children who need you and cherish the old.
God gives us the kingdom and calls us to labor
In ways that are fearless and loving and bold.

Don't fear, little flock, but take notice around you,
For right where you are, there is work you can do.
So sell what you have! With no wealth to confound you,
You'll find, undistracted: God's claim is on you!
In this world of suffering beyond human measure,
In this world of lying and violence and strife,
God gives us the kingdom; God gives us the treasure.
God gives us the Way and the Truth and the Life.

Biblical References: Luke 12:32-48; Matthew 6:19-21;
Matthew 24:42-45; Matthew 25:1-13
Tune: Traditional Welsh melody
Text: Copyright © 2016 by Carolyn Winfrey Gillette. All rights reserved.
Email: carolynshymns@gmail.com
New Hymns: www.carolynshymns.com

Reflection - Don't Fear, Little Flock

This hymn is based on Jesus' teaching, "Do not be afraid, little flock, for it is your Father's good pleasure to give you the kingdom" (Luke 12:32) It is part of "Singing In the Reign: A Worship Service Celebrating Jesus' Parables and Teachings in the Gospel of Luke. "

When I was in college, I never really found a home church in my college town; there was never one place I would regularly attend worship. I generally went to church somewhere. Sometimes I attended the United Methodist Church right on the edge of campus. Other times I tried out other churches with friends. I experienced Episcopal, Lutheran, Church of the Brethren, Roman Catholic, and independent/fundamentalist worship services, I heard diverse understandings of who Jesus is and what he wants us to be and to do.

There were times I heard sermons about how Jesus was a stern judge, someone we'd better look out for, someone to be feared if we didn't sign on to a certain set of 20 affirmations about God. Other churches said that if we would just repeat four or five sentences (ones that they would tell us, of course), we could avoid Jesus sending us to hell. Those churches were the ones I didn't go back to.

I am grateful for the times I went to worship and heard the good news of the gospel: "Do not be afraid, little flock, for it is your Father's good pleasure to give you the kingdom." Always, always, the grace of God comes first.

Still, there is a call to live a certain way in response to God's love in Jesus. We follow not out of fear, but out of gratitude. We are blessed to be a blessing.

—How have you experienced God as the One who delights in giving you the good gifts of love and forgiveness?

—How can Christians bless others by being careful not to accumulate too many possessions?

—How does simpler living benefit our neighbors?

__How does it help us to care for creation in the midst of a climate crisis?

—What are our "purses that never wear out"?

—What are the things that distract you from God's reign? How can you move them from the center of your life to a more appropriate place?

Chapter 13

Read Luke 13:1-9, including these words:

1 At that very time there were some present who told him about the Galileans whose blood Pilate had mingled with their sacrifices. 2 He asked them, "Do you think that because these Galileans suffered in this way they were worse sinners than all other Galileans? 3 No, I tell you; but unless you repent, you will all perish as they did. 4 Or those eighteen who were killed when the tower of Siloam fell on them—do you think that they were worse offenders than all the others living in Jerusalem? 5 No, I tell you; but unless you repent, you will all perish just as they did…" (Luke 13:1-5)

One Day the News was Grim
LEONI 6.6.8.4 ("The God of Abraham Praise")

One day, the news was grim:
Some people sought the Lord
To tell of Galileans
killed by Pilate's sword.
"Is anyone to blame?
Is this because they sinned?" —
Whenever there is trouble,
people ask again.

Then Jesus turned to say:
It's nothing they did wrong
that means their loved ones
now are singing mournful songs.
And yet you know it's true
that tragic things abound;
Since life is fragile, now's the time
to turn around!

O God, we pray for help
to see what we should change,
To see the values we ourselves
should rearrange.
Now help us know our sin,
the good we've left undone,
The times when you have looked for fruit
and we've borne none.

In Christ, we see your grace:
You give us one more day —
Another opportunity
to live your way.
May we again repent
and turn our lives to you,
And may we love our neighbors more
 and bear much fruit.

Biblical Reference: Luke 13:1-9
Tune: Traditional Hebrew melody
Text: Copyright © 2010 by Carolyn Winfrey Gillette.
All rights reserved.
Email: carolynshymns@gmail.com
New Hymns: www.carolynshymns.com

Reflection - One Day the News was Grim

This new hymn is also part of "Singing In the Reign," the worship service I wrote using a number of my hymns that are based on Jesus' parables. Jesus didn't try to explain why people were killed in the tragedy of a falling tower, or why some were killed when Pilate's troops interrupted their worship and killed them. Jesus used the occasion to point out that suffering is real. The reality of suffering points to our need to turn to God.

In our home, Bruce and I have an embroidered, framed wall hanging that a friend made years ago: "Life is fragile - Handle with prayer." Bruce and I have experienced the fragility of life in these past couple of years. In 2019, we learned that Bruce had acute leukemia. We spent two years dealing with hospitalizations, treatments, a bone marrow transplant, chemotherapy side effects, and many difficult days and nights. In that time, the pandemic also began and like many people dealing with compromised immune systems, we had to isolate ourselves as much as possible. As Bruce went through so much suffering, we learned to celebrate the gift of each new day.

The last line of the hymn is a prayer that we may "love our neighbors more and bear much fruit." Jesus showed love for his neighbors throughout his ministry; immediately after this teaching in Luke, he healed a woman (Luke 13:10-17).

—Do you try to explain why there is suffering, or do you simply try to get through it?
—What tragedies have you and your family faced?
—How have you responded to horrible events—personally, in your community, nationally, or globally?
—Who has helped you get through, day by day?

Read Luke 13:10-17:

10 Now he was teaching in one of the synagogues on the sabbath. 11 And just then there appeared a woman with a spirit that had crippled her for eighteen years. She was bent over and was quite unable to stand up straight. 12 When Jesus saw her, he called her over and said, "Woman, you are set free from your ailment." 13 When he laid his hands on her, immediately she stood up straight and began praising God. 14 But the leader of the synagogue, indignant because Jesus had cured on the sabbath, kept saying to the crowd, "There are six days on which work ought to be done; come on those days and be cured, and not on the sabbath day." 15 But the Lord answered him and said, "You hypocrites! Does not each of you on the sabbath untie his ox or his donkey from the manger, and lead it away to give it water? 16 And ought not this woman, a daughter of Abraham whom Satan bound for eighteen long years, be set free from this bondage on the sabbath day?" 17 When he said this, all his opponents were put to shame; and the entire crowd was rejoicing at all the wonderful things that he was doing.

That Woman in the Crowd
LEONI 6.6.8.4 ("The God of Abraham Praise")

That woman in the crowd —
she could not stand up tall;
Her back was bent, her head was bowed —
and Jesus saw!
That Sabbath day of rest,
he saw her misery;
He told her, "Woman, from your ailment
you are free!"

He saw another thing,
when others thought her odd;
He saw a child of Abraham,
a child of God!
And soon she saw it, too!
She must have been amazed!
She stood up tall and offered God
her thanks and praise.

A leader said, "You're wrong!"
for sin was what he saw.
He could not understand
this One who broke the law.
The Sabbath rules were strict
and work was not allowed —
not even when it healed a woman
bent and bowed.

Christ said, "What matters most?
What rules will you obey?
You care for ox and donkey
on the Sabbath day!"
For Jesus knew the truth —
 that people matter more,
And God loves things
that heal, encourage and restore.

What barriers do we build
to God's abundant grace?
Do we want church to be
a perfect, law-filled place?
Or will we dare to love —
to see what Jesus saw —
That God's great welcome matters more
than rule and law.

Biblical Reference: Luke 13:10-17
Tune: Traditional Hebrew melody
Text: Copyright © 2016 by Carolyn Winfrey Gillette.
All rights reserved.
Email: carolynshymns@gmail.com
New Hymns: www.carolynshymns.com

Reflection - That Woman in the Crowd

"That Woman in the Crowd" tells the story of Jesus healing a woman on the Sabbath and acknowledging that people matter more than rules. It is a healing story and so much more; it is a story of Jesus' "seeing" a woman with very real needs. The woman "could not stand up tall..." yet "Jesus saw..."

Some of the religious leaders saw something else. Instead of seeing a woman who was bent over and struggling, they saw laws being broken or bent. They were more focused on the law than on the human being who was hurt and needing healing.

I remember hearing, during The Great Recession in 2008, about a school cafeteria that was denying lunches to children because their families were behind in paying their lunch bills. At one point, a cafeteria worker handed a child a lunch tray and then realized that the family's lunch bill wasn't paid up; the worker snatched the tray out of the child's hand and threw the contents in the trash, then gave the child a pre-made peanut butter sandwich. Good food, already in a child's hands, ended up in a trash can because an adult was following the rules to the letter—and a child was embarrassed and confused.

Fortunately, the school employees I have known and worked with over the years have been very gracious to the children in their care. They are people who knowingly or unknowingly have followed the teachings of Jesus. During that same difficult economic time, a "lunch lady" told us that children were coming through the line saying, "My mom said to ask for a little extra because we don't have food at home for supper." That sweet cafeteria worker would pile on the vegetables, give the child a little extra meat, and then put an extra piece of fruit or bread on the tray for the child to take home. Later, many schools institutionalized these acts of kindness; they started providing free breakfast and lunch programs, or they arranged to send "To Go" backpacks of food home with hungry children on the weekends. For a while, though, hungry children depended on kind "cafeteria ladies" who were willing to break the rules.

Quite a few adults in churches remember, as children, hearing from children's choir directors: "You can't carry a tune in a bucket... the children's choir is not for you." Or "You just stand in the back and move your mouth." Those leaders may have followed the rules for producing good music— but some of those children never wanted lo sing again. Other directors, filled with grace, knew that all God's children had a place in the choir— where they could make mistakes, learn, and grow. In the words of the hymn,

"For Jesus knew the truth —
that people matter more,
And God loves things
that heal, encourage and restore."

—Are there times we put up barriers in front of people— by putting strict rules or expectations before grace?
—Are there ways we can be less rule-focused and more grace-filled in our churches?

Read Luke 13:31-35:

31 At that very hour some Pharisees came and said to him, "Get away from here, for Herod wants to kill you." 32 He said to them, "Go and tell that fox for me, 'Listen, I am casting out demons and performing cures today and tomorrow, and on the third day I finish my work. 33 Yet today, tomorrow, and the next day I must be on my way, because it is impossible for a prophet to be killed outside of Jerusalem.' 34 Jerusalem, Jerusalem, the city that kills the prophets and stones those who are sent to it! How often have I desired to gather your children together as a hen gathers her brood under her wings, and you were not willing! 35 See, your house is left to you. And I tell you, you will not see me until the time comes when you say, 'Blessed is the one who comes in the name of the Lord.'"

Lord, We Confess We Turn Away

TALLIS' CANON 8.8.8.8 ("All Praise to Thee, My God, This Night")

Lord, we confess we turn away
The very ones we need today.
God's prophets speak out loud and clear,
Yet prophets still aren't welcomed here.

You grieved for old Jerusalem
For you were like a mother hen
Who brought her brood beneath her wings —
While they were drawn to other things.

Lord, call us out and draw us in
when we would rather side with sin —
Let the prophetic things you say
still challenge how we live this day.

May we who listen to your voice,
Be still, be wise, then make a choice.
You call us to a life that's new;
Lord, may we now return to you.

Biblical Reference: Luke 13:31-35
Tune: Thomas Tallis, 1561
Text: Copyright © 2019 by Carolyn Winfrey Gillette.
All rights reserved.
Email: carolynshymns@gmail.com
New Hymns: www.carolynshymns.com

Reflection - Lord, We Confess We Turn Away

How frustrating it is for a loving parent— or for a grandparent who is raising a grandchild— when the child consistently doesn't listen and turns onto a dangerous path. How frustrating it must have been for Jesus to speak a message of love and to have people constantly trying to undercut his teaching or— perhaps worse— to simply ignore it. I wonder if Jesus weeps today, seeing how we turn away— in the words of this hymn, "drawn to other things."

Look at the prophets! God still sends prophets, and we turn away from them:

Local health care providers speak up about the need for vaccines, and there are people who won't listen, preferring to listen to random people on the Internet.

Climate scientists tell us we have just a few years to turn away from fossil fuels, and we keep on wasting energy because conserving resources is inconvenient for us.

We elect politicians who say the things we want to hear for our own benefit, instead of ones who promise to work for the common good.

Some states and localities are refusing to teach about racism in our nation's history because our history of racism makes people uncomfortable.

"Lord, call us out and draw us in
when we would rather side with sin —
Let the prophetic things you say
still challenge how we live this day."

—Which prophetic voices speaking the truth make you most uncomfortable?
—Which voices do you need to listen to today

Chapter 14

Read Luke 14:16-24, including these words:

…16 Then Jesus said to him, "Someone gave a great dinner and invited many. 17 At the time for the dinner he sent his slave to say to those who had been invited, 'Come; for everything is ready now.' 18 But they all alike began to make excuses…

21 So the slave returned and reported this to his master. Then the owner of the house became angry and said to his slave, 'Go out at once into the streets and lanes of the town and bring in the poor, the crippled, the blind, and the lame.' 22 And the slave said, 'Sir, what you ordered has been done, and there is still room.' 23 Then the master said to the slave, 'Go out into the roads and lanes, and compel people to come in, so that my house may be filled. 24 For I tell you, none of those who were invited will taste my dinner.'" (Luke 14:16-18, 21-24)

A King Planned a Party

ASH GROVE 6.6.11.6.6.11 D ("Let All Things Now Living")

A king planned a party — a feast, rich and hearty.
He sent invitations to all of his guests.
So what could be better than getting a letter
And being invited and welcomed and blessed?
"My work needs attention," said one, "Not to mention,
My family is growing. There's so much to do."
"My farm," said another, "Is big, and — oh, brother —
I'm busy with hobbies I want to pursue."

"The wedding is ready! My guests are not worthy!"
The king told his servants when nobody came.
So go search the alleys, the hills and the valleys,
And bring in the poor and the blind and the lame."
That day there was singing and halls that were ringing
With laughter and joy in that wonderful place.
For those who attended knew how they depended
Upon the king's generous mercy and grace.

O God, you invite us! You seek to delight us.
Your table is ready for those who say "Yes!"
Do we make excuses when you want to choose us
To sit at your table, forgiven and blessed?
And, Lord, as you welcome us into your kingdom,
May we reach to welcome the world by your grace.
You love the outsider. Now may we reach wider
To welcome the world with your loving embrace.

Biblical References: Matthew 22:1-14; Luke 14:16-24
Tune: Traditional Welsh melody
Text: Copyright © 2014 by Carolyn Winfrey Gillette.
All rights reserved.
Email: carolynshymns@gmail.com
New Hymns: www.carolynshymns.com

Reflection - A King Planned a Party

Who will eat bread in the kingdom of God? Who will be so blessed? Jesus heard the question, and so he told a story. The parable of The Great Dinner, or the Wedding Banquet, is the basis for this hymn. It can be found in Matthew 22:1-14 and Luke 14:16-24.

I once received an email note from a church that acted out this hymn, "A King Planned a Party," as they sang it in worship on a Sunday morning. In that small-town congregation, as the hymn was played and sung, worship leaders passed out "props"— a fast food restaurant paper crown for a king, papers rolled up to look like invitations for a few people at first, a "deed" for a farm, a stuffed-animal cow, and of course invitations to everyone at the end. The mayor of the town was visiting the church that Sunday, and after the worship service, he said joyfully, "We ought to sing more songs like this one!" I appreciated hearing about their creativity in playing with this hymn. Perhaps the mayor's delight was also about the wonderful message of Jesus' parable: No one is excluded. All are welcome at God's banquet feast. In the words of the hymn,

"You love the outsider. Now may we reach wider
To welcome the world with your loving embrace.

—Do you remember being a child and being the one person in a group who was not invited to a party?
—Do you remember a time when you thought you were not good enough, or smart enough, or popular enough, to go somewhere with others— and then you were enthusiastically welcomed in?
—How does your church practice hospitality?
—What efforts do you make to intentionally include people who may be considered "outsiders"?

Chapter 15

Read Luke 15:1-2:

15 Now all the tax collectors and sinners were coming near to listen to him. 2 And the Pharisees and the scribes were grumbling and saying, "This fellow welcomes sinners and eats with them."

Christ, You Are The Savior
ASH GROVE 6.6.11.6.6.11 D ("Let All Things Now Living")

Christ, you are the Savior, the Way to the Father,
The Truth we depend on, the Life that we need.
We trust you, believing! We listen, receiving
The joy of the gospel by which we are freed.
Yet, Lord, you remind us: Through mercy you find us,
By grace you forgive us. The way home is yours!
We dare not judge others, our sisters and brothers
Whom you choose to welcome through love's open doors.

With outcast and sinner you sat down to dinner;
You healed the Samaritans, Gentiles, too.
The poor knew your caring — the rich, your declaring
That God welcomes everyone, not just a few.
A conquering nation brought harsh occupation.
A soldier came asking; you offered a hand.
A thief saw your power in his final hour;
You welcomed him home to God's heavenly land.

O Lord, all around us, your mercies astound us
As others discover the Way you reveal.
A man whispers, "Help me!" A woman cries, "Mercy!"
A doubter discovers your welcome is real.
O Way to the Father, your mercy is broader
Than we as your people have often proclaimed.
May we welcome others as sisters and brothers,
And treasure the life that we share in your name.

Biblical References: John 14:6; Luke 15:2, 17:11-19, 7:1-10;
Mark 7:24-30; Luke 7:20-35, 23:39-43
Tune: Traditional Welsh melody
Text: Copyright © 2014 by Carolyn Winfrey Gillette. All rights reserved.
Email: carolynshymns@gmail.com
New Hymns: www.carolynshymns.com

Reflection - Christ, You Are The Savior

This hymn begins with an affirmation that Jesus is the Way, the Truth and the Life. It is based on a number of verses from Mark, Luke and John's gospels. Sometimes this statement of Jesus has been used as a "clobber" verse to shame or scare people who have not come to know God's love in Jesus Christ. The gospels remind us that the same Jesus who said, "I am the Way, the Truth and the Life" is the One who sat down to enjoy meals with people who were considered outcasts and sinners. When I was writing this hymn, I wove in a number of different biblical stories where Jesus welcomed people of different religions and nationalities.

We all choose the people we share meals with. From the lunchroom in the school cafeteria, to the break room at work, to the tables at the church potluck supper, we decide where we will sit down. Sometimes we sit down quickly at the nearest spot; sometimes we scan the room for a minute, looking for our friends. How often do we look for the person no one likes— the one who is grumpy or unpopular or hard to get along with? How often do we choose the one who has a reputation for being a troublemaker? We want to eat in our "safe spaces," and that is understandable. Yet, the gospel of Luke reminds us that Jesus sought out the outsiders who needed grace and forgiveness.

—Can you imagine the joy that the sinners and outcasts felt when they were invited and included by Jesus?
—Who can you invite to dinner?

Since Jesus is the Way and *he* ate with sinners, we know who we are called to have as our table companions. In the middle of a pandemic, it has been hard to share meals with our friends or with strangers. Many churches have canceled social events like church dinners in an effort to keep people safe. In November, in rural, Central New York State, on a chilly Sunday afternoon, our church members bundled up and had a tailgate party at Hickories Park, down by the river. We thought 20 people would show up on such a cold day. More than twice as many people came. We gathered together— friends, old and new neighbors, people from differing cultures, children, youth, adults. All were welcome in that place and around those tables.

During the pandemic, our congregation started meeting on Zoom for worship. After each Sunday worship service, we would stay online for a Zoom coffee hour. One of the best parts of coffee hour was the breakout rooms. The tech people would randomly assign us to small groups of three or four people. We soon realized that we were talking, in depth, to people we might have missed months earlier, when we were in the Fellowship Hall after worship.   On Zoom, people couldn't just sit down with their closest friends at a table in a building. Over many months of online coffee hours, the breakout rooms gave us wonderful opportunities to visit with a much wider variety of people.

—If times are unsafe, as in a pandemic surge or flu season, what are creative ways you can reach out and share conversation and food with people who need to be included?

Read Luke 15:3-10:

3 So he told them this parable: 4 "Which one of you, having a hundred sheep and losing one of them, does not leave the ninety-nine in the wilderness and go after the one that is lost until he finds it? 5 When he has found it, he lays it on his shoulders and rejoices. 6 And when he comes home, he calls together his friends and neighbors, saying to them, 'Rejoice with me, for I have found my sheep that was lost.' 7 Just so, I tell you, there will be more joy in heaven over one sinner who repents than over ninety-nine righteous persons who need no repentance.

8 "Or what woman having ten silver coins, if she loses one of them, does not light a lamp, sweep the house, and search carefully until she finds it? 9 When she has found it, she calls together her friends and neighbors, saying, 'Rejoice with me, for I have found the coin that I had lost.' 10 Just so, I tell you, there is joy in the presence of the angels of God over one sinner who repents."

Jesus' Wondrous Words of Grace

ST. GEORGE'S WINDSOR 7.7.7.7 D ("Come, Ye Thankful People, Come")

Jesus' wondrous words of grace
Welcome all to God's embrace:
Welcome if you're rich or poor,
If you're knocking at the door,
If you come from far away,
If you need a place to stay.
If you suffer want or pain,
You are welcome in God's reign!

Do you live in fear and doubt?
Do you seek to leave some out?
Do you think that some can't get
To the table God has set?
Think there is no room for you?
Jesus says you're welcome, too.
Think you're different, sinful, odd?
You are welcome, child of God!

Jesus says to all the church:
Welcome in the ones who search,
Welcome in the ones who mourn,
Welcome in the tired and worn,
Welcome those who live in fear,
Welcome in the sinners here.
As you do to these, you see,
So you also welcome me.

Biblical References: Matthew 5:46-48; Matthew 25:35-36;
Luke 14:15-24; Luke 15; John 3:16-17; Galatians 3:28;
Tune: George Job Elvey, 1856
Text: Copyright © 2018 by Carolyn Winfrey Gillette. All rights reserved.
Email: carolynshymns@gmail.com
New Hymns: www.carolynshymns.com

Reflection - Jesus' Wondrous Words of Grace

I wrote this hymn in 2018 in response to the increasing intolerance, hatred and prejudice that was happening in the United States. Because of political events and personalities, there was a growing acceptance in some circles of racism, sexism, and homophobia.

Look at the three wonderful lost and found stories in Luke 15. They begin with Jesus eating with outcasts and sinners. Some people saw Jesus' openness to being with sinners and murmured and complained about his dinner companions. Jesus told three parables that are recorded here in Luke 15: the parables of the lost sheep, the lost coin and the lost boy.

This hymn overflows with welcome, as Jesus' teachings do as well. Lately I have heard many people talk about how our country should "go back to the Bible," I hope they— and we— read the many wonderful biblical teachings about Jesus welcoming all people; some of these teachings are listed at the bottom of the hymn.

Look at each line of the hymn and see if you can fill in the name of a person you know who needs to know Jesus' welcome.

—What neighbor of your church is knocking at your door?
—What immigrant or refugee— or someone else new in the community— has come from far away?
—What family is struggling to pay rent?
—Who is sick or in pain, perhaps in a nursing home?
—Who in your community is having troubling saying, "I am a beloved child of God"?

Read Luke 15:11-32, including these words:

…31 Then the father said to him, 'Son, you are always with me, and all that is mine is yours. 32 But we had to celebrate and rejoice, because this brother of yours was dead and has come to life; he was lost and has been found.'" (Luke 15:31-32)

The Prodigal Son
ASH GROVE 6.6.11.6.6.11 D ("Let All Things Now Living")

"Can't wait till your deathbed! You might as well drop
dead!"
A son told his dad, "Give my share of this place."
His dad chose to give him some land that they lived on.
That son sold the land; it was quite a disgrace.
He went from that country and wasted the money.
There came a great drought; he was soon feeding swine.
Life gave him a beating; he longed to be eating
the pods in the pig yard at his dinnertime.

He lost his pretenses and came to his senses:
"The servants at home have it better than this."
The hurting son hurried, but still he was worried:
Would he be forgiven or killed or dismissed?
His dad said, "You're living!" and ran to forgive him;
he said, "Bring a ring and and a robe! Sandals, too!
Now make a feast ready! It's time for a party!
My son who was dead has a life that is new!"

The elder son, listening, heard music and dancing;
he heard that his brother had been welcomed home.
He stood outside, fuming, his anger consuming,
for he'd never had such a feast of his own.
"Your brother's returning is what I've been yearning,"
the father said, "He who was lost has been found."
So we, like that brother, must love one another,
for God is a parent whose mercy abounds.

Biblical Reference: Luke 15:1-3, 15:11b-32
Tune: Traditional Welsh melody
Text: Copyright © 2019 by Carolyn Winfrey Gillette. All rights reserved.
Email: carolynshymns@gmail.com
New Hymns: www.carolynshymns.com

Reflection - The Prodigal Son

Usually hymn titles come from the first line of a hymn.
I started this hymn with the implied message of the
younger son, "Can't wait for your deathbed!" When the
younger son asked his father for his inheritance, he was
basically saying, "I want to take the land you are living on,
the farm that you depend on, and I want to sell what will
be my share of it after you die." "Can't wait for your
deathbed!" was his message. This, however, did not seem
like the best hymn title, so I simply called this hymn, "The
Prodigal Son."

Can you imagine? Can you imagine the father's grief
when his son valued money and land more than the
father's well-being and security? If the father sold half his
land to give to his son, how would the father be able to
maintain his standard of living for the rest of his life? The
neighbors certainly understood the gravity of the situation.
What disrespect! They surely never wanted to see the son
again!

The second verse of the hymn is about the younger son
coming to his senses and returning home in fear, only to
find that his father runs to welcome him home. That is
grace. The father's forgiveness was a free gift for his son.
The son did nothing to deserve it. So God forgives us and
welcomes us home.

The third verse, of course, is about the older brother's
response. He, also, was lost— in his own way. For all
those years, since his younger brother had taken his
inheritance and gone away, the older one had worked
faithfully on his father's farm. His faithful service was
commendable— yet he lost his graciousness, compassion,
and mercy. He, too, needed to turn his life around and find
his father's welcome at the welcome party.

—When have you wandered away?

—When have you felt the relief of being fully forgiven?

—When have you been more concerned about rules, expectations and obligations than about offering grace and welcome?

—When have you resented someone who seemed to take advantage of a situation for personal gain?

— When have you offered grace and forgiveness? Was it a difficult thing to do?

Chapter 16

Read Luke 16:1-15, including these words:

1 Then Jesus said to the disciples, "There was a rich man who had a manager, and charges were brought to him that this man was squandering his property. 2 So he summoned him and said to him, 'What is this that I hear about you? Give me an accounting of your management, because you cannot be my manager any longer.' 3 Then the manager said to himself, 'What will I do, now that my master is taking the position away from me? I am not strong enough to dig, and I am ashamed to beg. 4 I have decided what to do so that, when I am dismissed as manager, people may welcome me into their homes.' 5 So, summoning his master's debtors one by one, he asked the first, 'How much do you owe my master?' 6 He answered, 'A hundred jugs of olive oil.' He said to him, 'Take your bill, sit down quickly, and make it fifty.' 7 Then he asked another, 'And how much do you owe?' He replied, 'A hundred containers of wheat.' He said to him, 'Take your bill and make it eighty.' 8 And his master commended the dishonest manager because he had acted shrewdly; for the children of this age are more shrewd in dealing with their own generation than are the children of light. 9 And I tell you, make friends for yourselves by means of dishonest wealth so that when it is gone, they may welcome you into the eternal homes… (Luke 16:1-9)

A Dishonest Steward

ASH GROVE 6.6.11.6.6.11 D ("Let All Things Now Living")

A dishonest steward found out he'd been fired;
he thought, "I'm in trouble! Now what will I do?
It's not very likely that I'll soon be hired,
so I'll make a plan to get out of this stew."
He called up the people who owed his boss money;
he settled their debts at deep discount that day.
Those debtors were thrilled that their day had turned
    sunny;
now they were indebted to him, in a way.

His boss heard what happened but did not reverse it;
His debtors were praising him; what could he do?
That boss seemed the hero; he'd make matters worse if
he tried to collect from those debtors anew.
He praised the shrewd worker — but not for deception;
he praised him for wisdom — for knowing the score.
He praised him for knowing that people could help him;
when money was gone, he'd have what mattered more.

O Lord, we remember the things that you taught us:
Though he was dishonest, that worker was shrewd.
He looked to the future and he was relentless.
He saw the big picture; he knew what was true.
For money won't matter; it never can save us.
Relationships matter when push comes to shove.
May we as a church face the changes around us —
Not trusting in money, but seeking to love.

Biblical Reference: Luke 16:1-15
Tune: Traditional Welsh melody ("Let All Things Now Living") (MIDI)
Text: Copyright © 2019 by Carolyn Winfrey Gillette. All rights reserved.
Email: carolynshymns@gmail.com
New Hymns: www.carolynshymns.com

Reflection - A Dishonest Steward

This is a parable that makes many of us uncomfortable. Why would Jesus commend a person who was less-than-ethical in his business dealings? It doesn't make sense, at first.

Jesus pointed here to someone who was driven to pursue a goal.   What the dishonest steward realized was that all the money in the world wouldn't protect him when he eventually faced trouble. When he lost his job, there would be no financial safety net to catch him. Relationships… friendships… would be much more valuable than money. If even a scoundrel could recognize that, why shouldn't Christians understand it, too?

Jesus talked a lot about money. Sometimes he told people to give away their money and possessions— but not always. He commended Zacchaeus for promising to give away *half* his money. Jesus' conversations about wealth were not always the same. He understood that different people would use and relate to money in different ways. Yet he always, always, stressed the importance of putting people before possessions.

—What is your relationship with money? What role does it play in your life? How much do you depend on it?
—What are your total assets?
—What are your social assets? Are there people you can call on at three in the morning if you need help?
—Do others know that they could call on you at three in the morning if they needed your assistance in an emergency?

Read Luke 16:19-31, including these words:

19 "There was a rich man who was dressed in purple and fine linen and who feasted sumptuously every day. 20 And at his gate lay a poor man named Lazarus, covered with sores, 21 who longed to satisfy his hunger with what fell from the rich man's table; even the dogs would come and lick his sores… (Luke 16:19-21)

Outside My Gate, Outside My Door
O WALY WALY 8.8.8.8 ("Though I May Speak")

Outside my gate, outside my door,
is someone there who's lost or poor?
Is someone there I do not see —
that I walk by — who has a need?

Is there a child who longs for care?
An older friend who needs a prayer?
Someone who seeks a helping hand?
A refugee new to this land?

Outside our church, is someone near
who cries in pain, who lives in fear?
Is someone close who has no way
to buy the food she needs this day?

Some gates are made of wood or stone,
And some are made of sin alone.
Some doors are made of greed and pride;
they also keep the poor outside.

As we look out, Christ, may we see
our common, shared humanity.
May we kneel down and serve you more
outside our gate, outside our door.

Biblical Reference: Luke 16:19-31
Tune: Traditional English melody
Email: carolynshymns@gmail.com
New Hymns: www.carolynshymns.com

Reflection - Outside My Gate, Outside My Door

"Outside My Gate, Outside My Door" is a hymn about poor Lazarus outside the rich man's gate (Luke 16:19-31). Martin Luther King, Jr., retold this story in his final sermon before he was assassinated.

There's been a lot of talk in the news lately, reminding us that the rich are getting richer while the poor are getting poorer. It's easy to look up the latest statistics online and to see that income inequality has become a huge problem. Many individuals and heads of households are working full-time jobs, and yet they cannot afford to pay for the basics of rent, food, clothing, medical care and school supplies for their children. Minimum wage jobs simply do not pay enough money.

It is easy to blame the top one percent and to say they are the ones who are like the rich man in the story. When we think about it, though, many of us have experienced the vast differences in people's economic conditions— and many of us are on the side that has plenty. On a church mission trip in Honduras, I was with a group of people who, after a long week in a rural community, were sitting in a city restaurant, enjoying a wonderful meal. As we were eating, hungry children stood outside the restaurant window by our table and reached their hands through the iron grating on the windows, desperately asking us for something to eat— a roll, a piece of meat, anything. A few days after I came home from Honduras, I went to one of those big box stores in my town and found myself overwhelmed by the high shelves filled with huge boxes of food. May the words of the hymn be our prayer:

"May we kneel down and serve you more
outside our gate, outside our door."

—When have you been overwhelmed by the economic

and social inequalities around you?

—When have you sought to ignore them for a while?

—In what ways do we separate ourselves or our neighborhoods from others— with gates, highways, staff members who act as gatekeepers, or in other ways?

—Who is outside your gate, literally or figuratively, right now?

—What is Jesus calling you to do?

Chapter 17

Read Luke 17:11-19:

11 On the way to Jerusalem Jesus was going through the region between Samaria and Galilee. 12 As he entered a village, ten lepers approached him. Keeping their distance, 13 they called out, saying, "Jesus, Master, have mercy on us!" 14 When he saw them, he said to them, "Go and show yourselves to the priests." And as they went, they were made clean. 15 Then one of them, when he saw that he was healed, turned back, praising God with a loud voice. 16 He prostrated himself at Jesus' feet and thanked him. And he was a Samaritan. 17 Then Jesus asked, "Were not ten made clean? But the other nine, where are they? 18 Was none of them found to return and give praise to God except this foreigner?" 19 Then he said to him, "Get up and go on your way; your faith has made you well."

Ten Who Suffered Sought Out Jesus
BEACH SPRING 8.7.8.7 D ("God Whose Giving Knows No Ending")

Ten who suffered sought out Jesus
when they saw him traveling through:
"Jesus, Master, show your mercy!
Hear our cry, we beg of you!"
When he saw them, Jesus answered,
"Find the priests. See what they say."
As they did what Jesus told them,
ten found healing on the way.

Ten were healed, and saw the wonder!
Nine kept going, homeward bound.
Only one — despised by others —
took the time to turn around.
Finding Jesus, singing praises,
he said, "Thank you!" on that day.
Jesus said, "Your faith has healed you.
But the others — where are they?"

Where are we, O God of mercy?
For your Son has blessed us, too.
He has given life abundant,
offered healing, made us new.
Like the nine, are we distracted
by our homes, our work, our play?
Or do we return and thank you,
taking time to humbly pray?

Jesus, make us truly grateful
for the blessings we receive.
Like that one, may we say, "Thank you!"
like that one, may we believe:
Give us faith to see your mercy,
and through all we do and say,
May our lives become our "thank you!"
as we follow you each day.

Biblical Reference: Luke 17:11-19
Tune: *The Sacred Harp*, 1844; attributed to Benjamin Franklin White
Text: Copyright © 2014 by Carolyn Winfrey Gillette.
All rights reserved.
Email: carolynshymns@gmail.com
New Hymns: www.carolynshymns.com

Reflection - Ten Who Suffered Sought Out Jesus

This hymn celebrates the story of Jesus healing ten people. One, a Samaritan, an outsider, came back to say, "Thank you!" for the blessing that he had received. This traditional story of thankfulness is one that often makes its way into worship services around Thanksgiving.

I am intrigued by Jesus' words in Luke 17:19: "Get up and go on your way; your faith has made you well." Jesus gives us the gift of healing. Sometimes, our very attempts to say, "Thank you!" contribute to the healing that takes place.

I remember, years ago, talking with a friend who was going through a rough time. One day, she started making a list of all the things that she was thankful for in her life. The very act of making the list was a turning point, as she realized God was still working in wonderful ways in her life. Years later, I was volunteering at a group home for teenage girls, doing some creative writing projects with them. One of their assignments was to keep a gratitude journal. In their troubled lives, they began to look for even the smallest things for which they could be thankful— a special lunch, a sunny day, a friend's kindness, a visit with a sibling in foster care. We had some good conversations that were opportunities for healing.

Once when Bruce and I were grieving the departure of our beloved foster son who left our home suddenly, someone gave us the good advice to add something of beauty to our lives. The person suggested we buy a painting, redecorate a room, or plant flowers. We planted lots and lots of flowers that spring— more than we had ever planted before— right by the driveway. As we tended the flowers and walked past them regularly, we found ourselves saying, "Thank you!" to God. We also saw the flowers and thought of our former foster son and prayed for him.

—When has Jesus worked to bring healing to you?
—When have your "thank you's" been part of your healing?
—When have you seen Jesus bringing healing to people on the outside looking in?

Chapter 18

Read Luke 18:1-8:

1 Then Jesus told them a parable about their need to pray always and not to lose heart. 2 He said, "In a certain city there was a judge who neither feared God nor had respect for people. 3 In that city there was a widow who kept coming to him and saying, 'Grant me justice against my opponent.' 4 For a while he refused; but later he said to himself, 'Though I have no fear of God and no respect for anyone, 5 yet because this widow keeps bothering me, I will grant her justice, so that she may not wear me out by continually coming.'" 6 And the Lord said, "Listen to what the unjust judge says. 7 And will not God grant justice to his chosen ones who cry to him day and night? Will he delay long in helping them? 8 I tell you, he will quickly grant justice to them. And yet, when the Son of Man comes, will he find
faith on earth?"

God, You Hear Our Weary Praying

BEACH SPRING 8.7.8.7 D ("God Whose Giving
Knows No Ending")

God, you hear our weary praying,
and you know that we lose heart.
All around we see the suffering
of a world that's torn apart.
We see leaders of the nations
filled with arrogance and greed.
We see friends and family hurting,
facing overwhelming need.

God, we cannot help but wonder:
Do our prayers do any good?
Do they change the nations' leaders?
Do they change our neighborhood?
Why do loved ones keep on suffering
when they're in our constant prayer?
Do you hear the cries we're offering?
Are you listening? Are you there?

Then you teach us of this woman:
She was widowed; she was poor.
"Grant me justice!" she kept calling
at an unjust judge's door.
Though that judge respected no one,
he was no match for her cries.
He responded to her pleading,
granting justice, changing lives.

How much more is your compassion!
God, you're just and good and fair.
May we lift to you our sorrows
and the burdens that we bear.
May we pray, for you reign o'er us!
May we ask — for you are kind!
May we trust that you will help us
in your goodness, in your time.

Biblical Reference: Luke 18:1-8
Tune: *The Sacred Harp*, 1844; attributed to Benjamin Franklin White
Text: Copyright © 2019 by Carolyn Winfrey Gillette.
Email: carolynshymns@gmail.com
New Hymns: www.carolynshymns.com

Reflection - God, You Hear Our Weary Praying

"God, You Hear Our Weary Praying" is based on Jesus' parable of the widow and the unjust judge; it is a reminder for us to pray and not lose heart. I wrote this hymn in 2019 when many good people were losing heart as we saw people in our society filled with arrogance and greed. Every time we turned on the news, we heard another story about lies and distortions, immigrants being deported, children being separated from their parents at the border, life-saving benefits being taken away from people who were poor, and emboldened racism in our society. Many of us were growing weary. We prayed and we prayed, but we could not see an answer to our prayers. In the words of the hymn,

'God, we cannot help but wonder:
Do our prayers do any good?
Do they change the nations' leaders?
Do they change our neighborhood?"

In this story of the widow and the unjust judge, Jesus calls us to keep on praying. God wants us to be persistent in asking for the things we need. We don't know how our prayers make a difference. Maybe God will change the mind of another person who has been particularly greedy or cruel. Maybe God will change us, giving us strength and persistence to keep calling our Senators and Representatives about immigration issues, to keep on marching in the streets for racial justice, or to keep on going to the elementary school to mentor children, or to help refugees fleeing violence— even when we're tired.

—What problems in our world lead you to feeling worn out in your praying?
—How have your persistent prayers changed a situation?
— How have they changed you?

The hymn ends with these words:

"May we trust that you will help us
in your goodness, in your time."

—When you pray about something big like climate change,
immigration, racism and war— when you pray persistently,
every day, never ceasing— are there ways that you
understand God is answering your prayers?

Read Luke 18:9-14:

9 He also told this parable to some who trusted in themselves that they were righteous and regarded others with contempt: 10 "Two men went up to the temple to pray, one a Pharisee and the other a tax collector. 11 The Pharisee, standing by himself, was praying thus, 'God, I thank you that I am not like other people: thieves, rogues, adulterers, or even like this tax collector. 12 I fast twice a week; I give a tenth of all my income.' 13 But the tax collector, standing far off, would not even look up to heaven, but was beating his breast and saying, 'God, be merciful to me, a sinner!' 14 I tell you, this man went down to his home justified rather than the other; for all who exalt themselves will be humbled, but all who humble themselves will
be exalted."

A Pharisee Was Praying
AURELIA 7.6.7.6 D ("The Church's One Foundation")

A Pharisee was praying;
he proudly stood alone:
"God, thank you that I'm better
than others I have known."
He saw the faults of others,
yet in that holy place,
He missed the joy and wonder
of God's amazing grace.

Far off in that same Temple,
a tax collector stood.
He knew he was a sinner;
he knew that God is good.
"Have mercy, God, upon me!"
the tax collector cried.
He left that place of worship
forgiven, justified.

O God of love, forgive us
when we look all around
And think that, by our actions,
we stand on solid ground:
We pray, "See how we serve you!
We work and volunteer!
Aren't we the ones whose giving
builds up your kingdom here?"

May we, your church, be humble
in serving you each day,
For pride will never help us
to walk your kingdom-way.
May we know your forgiveness —
our need for mercy, too —
That, loved and loving others,
our life may be in you.

Biblical Reference: Luke 18:9-14
Tune: Samuel Sebastian Wesley, 1864
Text: Copyright © 2013 by Carolyn Winfrey Gillette.
Email: carolynshymns@gmail.com
New Hymns: www.carolynshymns.com

Reflection - A Pharisee Was Praying

One of the problems we have in reading the Bible is that we often put ourselves into the stories in the role of the "good people." Like the Pharisee in the Temple, we trust in our selves as the righteous ones and we view other people with contempt. Some might say that's human nature. Still, this kind of thinking gets in the way of healthy relationships with God and with each other.

It's not just the Pharisee who had to be wary of piety. Sometimes we stand alone, at a distance from others, and we are quick to criticize them.

This is true not just on a personal level but as a society, too. The more we separate ourselves from others, the less we understand them and the quicker we will be to criticize them. Our gated communities and divided neighborhoods make it harder for us to find times and places to interact with people from different racial ethnic and economic backgrounds.

—What are the ways you pull away from God and neighbor, as the neighbor stood apart from others?
—What are the ways you participate in the sins of our society— such as racism, classism and consumerism?
—Is there anyone you view with contempt?
—What do you need to be honest to God about today?

Read Luke 18:18-30, including these words:

18 A certain ruler asked him, "Good Teacher, what must I do to inherit eternal life?" 19 Jesus said to him, "Why do you call me good? No one is good but God alone. 20 You know the commandments: 'You shall not commit adultery; You shall not murder; You shall not steal; You shall not bear false witness; Honor your father and mother.'" 21 He replied, "I have kept all these since my youth." 22 When Jesus heard this, he said to him, "There is still one thing lacking. Sell all that you own and distribute the money to the poor, and you will have treasure in heaven; then come, follow me." 23 But when he heard this, he became sad; for he was very rich… (Luke 18:18-23)

Lord, What Must I Do?
LYONS 10.10.11.11 ("O Worship the King, All Glorious Above!")

"Lord, what must I do?" A man asked one day.
The kingdom of God still seemed far away.
Christ spoke with compassion, "Just do one thing more;
Sell all your possessions, and give to the poor ... "

The man was upset and started to grieve;
Did he even hear what he would receive?
For Jesus continued, " ... Then come, follow me,
And you will have treasure in heaven! You'll see!"

O Lord, we have much and so we confess
Wealth gets in the way; possessions possess!
Our money distorts how we hear your good news;
It changes our vision, obscuring our views.

O Lord, may we have the courage today
To get rid of all that gets in your way;
And may the impossible now be found true:
By grace, we are blest and find treasure in you.

Biblical References: Matthew 19:16-30; Mark 10:17-31; Luke 18:18-30
Tune: Joseph Martin Kraus, 1784; until recently attributed to Johann
Michael Haydn Text: Copyright © 2013 by Carolyn Winfrey Gillette. All
rights reserved.
Email: carolynshymns@gmail.com
New Hymns: www.carolynshymns.com

Reflection - Lord, What Must I Do?

What do you do, when the reign of God seems far away? What do you do when you feel disconnected from God? It is easy to get discouraged. For the man in this biblical story, the reign of God seemed to be a distant thing— like an inheritance that was far out of reach, one that he might never inherit. Jesus gave him an answer: In the words of the hymn,

"Christ spoke with compassion,
'Just do one thing more;
Sell all your possessions,
and give to the poor ...'"

We may have the same reaction as the person in the story. He was upset, and many of us would be, too. These words of Jesus ring in our ears so loudly and they are so jarring that we don't hear the promise that comes next: "You will have treasure in heaven." Good, lasting things will come to us when we give generously.

It's true that, in giving, we receive. In the midst of the pandemic, our congregation and others welcomed an Afghan family into our community. In a time when people were physically isolating themselves in their homes, we managed to furnish a house, welcome the family, help them with shopping, tutor their children, take them to medical appointments and more. Masks and vaccines helped church members and friends to be safe enough to reach out and provide a welcome. Over many months, we have found the treasure that comes from offering hospitality and being in relationship with new friends; the family has offered us their wonderful hospitality, too. We are learning from each other. We are all blessed.

The easiest thing to do during a world health crisis would have been to pull ourselves inward, to say, "We don't have anything left to give," and to say,"We don't know what tomorrow will bring. We have to guard our resources." Instead we found the treasures of neighbor reaching out to neighbor— giving and receiving love. We found the treasure of God's love. We can pray, in the words of the hymn,

"And may the impossible now be found true:
By grace, we are blest and find treasure in you."

—What kind of sacrificial giving is Jesus calling you to as an individual?
—What kind of sacrificial giving is Jesus calling you to as a church?
—When have you gotten just the smallest preview of treasure in heaven?

Read Luke 18:35-43:

35 As he approached Jericho, a blind man was sitting by the roadside begging. 36 When he heard a crowd going by, he asked what was happening. 37 They told him, "Jesus of Nazareth is passing by." 38 Then he shouted, "Jesus, Son of David, have mercy on me!" 39 Those who were in front sternly ordered him to be quiet; but he shouted even more loudly, "Son of David, have mercy on me!" 40 Jesus stood still and ordered the man to be brought to him; and when he came near, he asked him, 41 "What do you want me to do for you?" He said, "Lord, let me see again." 42 Jesus said to him, "Receive your sight; your faith has saved you." 43 Immediately he regained his sight and followed him, glorifying God; and all the people, when they saw it, praised God.

Jesus, Have Mercy!
BUNESSAN 5.5.5.4 D ("Morning Has Broken")

"Jesus, have mercy! Help! Son of David!"
So Bartimaeus called to the Lord.
Filled with great faith, he knew as he waited:
Christ was his hope for vision restored.

Jesus, have mercy! May we see clearly
You gave a gift we cannot repay.
You had it all, but loving us dearly,
Even your life, Lord, you gave away.

Jesus, have mercy when we're uncertain,
Hiding our talents high on our shelves.
As we've been blessed, may we be an offering —
Healing your world by giving ourselves.

Jesus, have mercy! May we give freely
So that the church has plenty to share.
May we bring tithes and offerings gladly,
Reaching to those in need everywhere.

Jesus, have mercy! Give us new vision;
Show us new ways to build up your church.
We are your people, called into mission!
Help us to bring your hope to the earth.

Biblical References: Mark 10:46-52; Philippians 2:5-11;
Matthew 25:11-30; Luke 18:35-43; Matthew 25:31-46;
2 Corinthians 8:1-15; Psalm 65:5
Email: carolynshymns@gmail.com
New Hymns: www.carolynshymns.com

Reflection - Jesus, Have Mercy!

This hymn celebrates Jesus' healing of a man who was blind. I wrote this hymn based on Mark's version of the healing story (Mark 10:46-52), in which the blind man is identified as Bartimaeus. In Luke, he is not named, yet the story is almost identical to Mark's story of the healing of Bartimaeus, so I have included the hymn here, in this book of hymns related to Luke. If you are using the hymn in worship with Luke's version of the story, you are welcome to change the second line, "So Bartimaeus called to the Lord..." to read, "One day a blind man called to the Lord." Or, you may want simply to point out the similarities and differences between Mark's and Luke's telling of the story. Either way, this hymn is a prayer that the church today will have a new vision of faithful living and service.

The man who was blind experienced a miracle— the gift of restored physical sight. Even before his physical sight was restored, though, he had spiritual insight. He knew to ask for help from Jesus.

It's interesting to me that the people around the blind man told him to be quiet. Throughout my ministry, I have noticed times when communities have basically told people who are hurting to be quiet. A town we lived in once tried to shut down a food pantry that was a joint effort of several churches in the community. A neighboring church struggled with the question of whether to continue to allow AA groups to meet in their building. When my husband and I were foster parents, a social worker once told us to be quiet about a foster child's needs because our reporting of past abuse meant she had to fill out extra paperwork.

—Are there times we prefer peace and serenity to justice and healing?

The blind man was persistent in seeking help. When the crowd told him to be quiet, he shouted all the more, asking Jesus to help him. Then Jesus asked this seeker a question: "What do you want me to do for you?"

—Are there times when you have been persistent in advocating for your own needs?
—Who was the person that you asked for help?
—Imagine Jesus asking you this question today. How would you answer it What do you want Jesus to do for you?

Chapter 19

Read Luke 19:1-10:

1He entered Jericho and was passing through it. 2 A man was there named Zacchaeus; he was a chief tax collector and was rich. 3 He was trying to see who Jesus was, but on account of the crowd he could not, because he was short in stature. 4 So he ran ahead and climbed a sycamore tree to see him, because he was going to pass that way. 5 When Jesus came to the place, he looked up and said to him, "Zacchaeus, hurry and come down; for I must stay at your house today." 6 So he hurried down and was happy to welcome him. 7 All who saw it began to grumble and said, "He has gone to be the guest of one who is a sinner." 8 Zacchaeus stood there and said to the Lord, "Look, half of my possessions, Lord, I will give to the poor; and if I have defrauded anyone of anything, I will pay back four times as much." 9 Then Jesus said to him, "Today salvation has come to this house, because he too is a son of Abraham. 10 For the Son of Man came to seek out and to save the lost."

Zacchaeus Was a Tax Man
AURELIA 7.6.7.6 D ("The Church's One Foundation")

Zacchaeus was a tax man
who one day climbed a tree,
For he was short in stature
and said he could not see.
And yet he had a problem
that mattered even more:
He didn't see the suffering
his greed had caused the poor.

O Lord, you saw Zacchaeus —
so wealthy, yet alone.
You said, "Come down — and hurry!
I'm coming to your home."
For you broke bread with sinners
and saw within each one
A person loved and treasured —
God's daughter or God's son.

It wasn't just the treetop
that helped Zacchaeus see;
Your love and welcome showed him
how different life could be.
He said that he'd start over
and work to make things fair;
He'd speak the truth, bring justice,
and find new ways to share.

O Christ, you bid us welcome
and help us all to see!
May we respond by building
a just society.
Then children won't be hungry
and all will share your bread.
Then those who now must struggle ·
will live in joy instead.

Biblical Reference: Luke 19:1-10
Tune: Samuel Sebastian Wesley, 1864
Text: Copyright © 2010 by Carolyn Winfrey Gillette.
All rights reserved.
Email: carolynshymns@gmail.com
New Hymns: www.carolynshymns.com

Reflection - Zacchaeus Was a Tax Man

I originally wrote this hymn to support Bread for the World's 2010 Offering of Letters that urged Congress to adopt changes to U.S. tax policy that would benefit low-income families.

Many Christians grew up singing "Zacchaeus was a wee little man," a children's song that celebrates this beloved story of Jesus and a tax collector. This hymn lifts up other aspects of the story beyond Zacchaeus' height; it celebrates Jesus' love for everyone and the call for his followers to work for justice for all.

This hymn is another example in Luke's gospel of Jesus reaching out to a sinner. When Zacchaeus heard that Jesus invited himself to dinner, he was amazed at the grace that Jesus was showing him. His response was to commit to living a new life. It wasn't just a new belief or thought process. Zacchaeus promised that he would live differently. He was wealthy; he would give a large portion of his possessions away.

Note that Zaccheaus' response to changing his life and giving away his wealth was one of joy. He knew that his money was best used to bring justice to others.

—When has someone been gracious and kind to you, offering to share a meal with you?
—What was your response?
—How can you use material resources to respond in gratitude to Jesus and to bring justice for others?

Read Luke 19:12-27:

12 So he said, "A nobleman went to a distant country to get royal power for himself and then return. 13 He summoned ten of his slaves, and gave them ten pounds, and said to them, 'Do business with these until I come back.' 14 But the citizens of his country hated him and sent a delegation after him, saying, 'We do not want this man to rule over us.' 15 When he returned, having received royal power, he ordered these slaves, to whom he had given the money, to be summoned so that he might find out what they had gained by trading. 16 The first came forward and said, 'Lord, your pound has made ten more pounds.' 17 He said to him, 'Well done, good slave! Because you have been trustworthy in a very small thing, take charge of ten cities.' 18 Then the second came, saying, 'Lord, your pound has made five pounds.' 19 He said to him, 'And you, rule over five cities.' 20 Then the other came, saying, 'Lord, here is your pound. I wrapped it up in a piece of cloth, 21 for I was afraid of you, because you are a harsh man; you take what you did not deposit, and reap what you did not sow.'" (Luke 19:12-21)

O God, We Yearn for Safety
ANGEL'S STORY 7.6.7.6 D ("O Jesus, I Have Promised")

O God, we yearn for safety; we long to be secure.
Yet faithful, loving service is what you value more.
You give us what is needed; you love, forgive and save.
Then, sending us to serve you, you call us to be brave.

You give to some ten talents — to others, two or three;
To some you give one blessing to manage faithfully.
For you, O Lord, are loving and don't demand success;
You daily call your people to lives of faithfulness.

You give your church the gospel — good news for us to share.
You give us great compassion for neighbors everywhere.
You give us skills to serve you and loving work to do.
We're blest to be a blessing, and called to risk for you.

O God, it seems much safer to live from day to day,
Protecting what you lend us and hiding it away.
Yet all these gifts can't flourish when hidden in the ground;
When we are brave to share them your blessings will abound.

Biblical References: Matthew 25:14-30; Luke 19:12-27
Tune: Arthur Henry Mann, 1888
Text: Copyright © 2011 by Carolyn Winfrey Gillette.
All rights reserved.
Email: carolynshymns@gmail.com
New Hymns: www.carolynshymns.com

Reflection - O God, We Yearn for Safety

Matthew and Luke tell the story of the talents in somewhat different ways, but the basic message is the same. We are called to trust our loving God *so much* that we are willing to take risks to follow God's way of love.

My mother used to say she grew up in a family that didn't take risks. It took me a while to understand this. For a long time, as I listened to the stories she told of my grandparents, I thought they were rather adventurous people for their time. When my mother's father was a teenager, he quit school and bought a train ticket, using the money he had saved to travel as far west as he could go. He got a job on a farm and worked there until he raised money for another train ticket, and he repeated this a number of times. This is how he traveled across the country. When he was a young man, he became an acrobat in a small circus. As an adult, he worked as a carpenter, and he would sometimes stand on his hands on chimney tops to entertain neighboring children. Likewise, my grandmother got a job as a teacher, and (though it was uncommon to do so) convinced the principal to "keep her on" as a teacher even after she got married. She dared to do what was unheard of in her day. These were people who knew how to take risks!

Later, though, I understood what my mother meant. Her parents were from a generation of white Americans who did not want to confront racism; they just accepted the social norms of the day. My mother told me that one time, when she was a girl, she wanted to invite some of her friends over to the house for a special activity, but my grandparents were concerned because one of the girls was Black. They were not ready to go against the racist culture they were living in. My mother was disappointed; she wanted all of her friends to be together. She ended up telling all of the ones she had invited that she wasn't allowed to have them over; they all went to another girl's house for the afternoon instead.

Jesus taught us that God gives each of us talents; when we use these gifts, we live life to the fullest. Usually we think of talents as things we do well. We may have musical talents, or talents for figuring out finances or building things. Or we think of talents as money (as in the parable)— something we should use wisely, invest and tithe. What if our talents are simply measures of love? What if my grandfather, who could stand on his hands on a chimney-top, had stood by the door and welcomed in my mother's friends— all of them? What if my grandmother, who had had the courage to advocate for herself, telling the school principal she wanted to continue to teach, had been brave enough to speak to the people who would not have approved of their daughter's Black friend coming to the house? What if they had used their talents— their measures of love— for the good of others?

It's not just my grandparents' generation that longed for safety, of course. We do the same thing. I wonder, sometimes, what our grandchildren will say about us when they look back on *our* lives. Maybe they will comment: "It's hard to believe they didn't pay much attention to their carbon footprint!" Or maybe they'll say, "Can you imagine they lived in a time when our country turned away refugees? I wonder if they spoke up about it" Or, "They knew there were immigrant children being snatched from their parents, and they did nothing!" Or, "They had a chance to protect voting rights and they squandered it away!"

Or maybe they will say, "I wonder, why didn't they welcome a transgender youth into their home from foster care?" Maybe they will ask, "What were they trying to do, play it safe?" What will our grandchildren say about us?

There are plenty of times I long for safety. There are times I have protected myself from honest conversations with difficult people. There are situations when I have not had the courage to speak out for what is right. There are days I have known what to do, and I have not done it.   There have been times when I was concerned that God was like a harsh nobleman; since I couldn't do something completely right, I didn't try to do the good thing at all.

When we hold back— when we refuse to risk money, talents, compassion, convenience, time or love— our lives are diminished. When we are willing to set aside our need for people to agree with us or like us, or for life to be convenient and easy— life may get considerably more difficult. Yes, maybe the people around us won't think well of us! Yet it's in those times— when we do our best, when we take a risk to try something new, when we let ourselves trust, when we make a decision to do what is moral and ethical and loving— it's in those times, in the words of the hymn,

When we are brave to share them your blessings will abound.

—When have you taken a risk to help someone else or to do what is just and merciful?
—What measures of love have you been brave to share?

Read Luke 19: 28-34:

28 After he had said this, he went on ahead, going up to Jerusalem. 29 When he had come near Bethphage and Bethany, at the place called the Mount of Olives, he sent two of the disciples, 30 saying, "Go into the village ahead of you, and as you enter it you will find tied there a colt that has never been ridden. Untie it and bring it here. 31 If anyone asks you, 'Why are you untying it?' just say this, 'The Lord needs it.'" 32 So those who were sent departed and found it as he had told them. 33 As they were untying the colt, its owners asked them, "Why are you untying the colt?" 34 They said, "The Lord needs it."

Two Disciples, Sent by Jesus

HOLY MANNA 8.7.8.7 D ("God, Who Stretched the Spangled Heavens")

Two disciples, sent by Jesus,
entered into one small town.
There they spied a colt still standing
where Christ said it would be found.
Two disciples asked to use it
and its owners soon agreed.
They responded to the calling
when they heard the Lord had need.

Jesus rode into the city,
there amid the cheering crowd.
Many people sang, "Hosanna!"
"Come and save!" they cried out loud.
People laid their cloaks before him
as the Lord was passing by;
many honored him as Savior,
as the Lord rode on to die.

On that Thursday, in the garden,
Jesus said, "Now, stay awake."
Yet they could not keep their vigil,
even for their Savior's sake.
One betrayed him, one denied him;
many felt great fear and loss.
One was made to walk beside him
and to carry Jesus' cross.

One lone man and several women
stayed and watched, as Jesus died.
Someone offered up a tomb there
after Christ was crucified.
All these ordinary people
witnessed such a mighty thing.
May we, too, see our salvation
in our suffering servant King.

Biblical References: Luke 19:28-40; Luke 22-23
Tune: William Moore's *Columbian Harmony*, 1825
Text: Copyright © 2019 by Carolyn Winfrey Gillette.
All rights reserved.
Email: carolynshymns@gmail.com
New Hymns: www.carolynshymns.com

Reflection - Two Disciples, Sent By Jesus

This hymn gives the whole sweeping story of Palm Sunday and Holy Week. It moves from adoration to accusation and from celebration to crucifixion.

The biblical story and the hymn both begin with a couple of Jesus' disciples simply doing what Jesus asked them to do. Jesus instructed them to go and find a colt, to ask the owners if they could borrow it, and to bring it to Jesus. In the words of the hymn,

"Two disciples, sent by Jesus,
entered into one small town.
There, they spied a colt still standing
where Christ said it would be found.
Two disciples asked to use it
and its owners soon agreed.
They responded to the calling
when they heard the Lord had need."

Sometimes following Jesus involves huge things. Other times, though, it's simply a matter of running errands. So much of my church work over the years has been about running errands: dropping off food for an inner city nonprofit's breakfast, meeting with someone about using our church space, borrowing supplies for a summer Vacation Bible School, helping to run off song sheets for the Christmas carol singing. Sometimes these things seem like chores. It can be hard to think of them as ministry.

Yet they are a good part of what our Christian service is all about. These little tasks are part of the overarching picture of what needs to be done. The disciples found a donkey for Jesus to ride. We may find a ride for the homeless family whose car breaks down in front of the church.

Always, in whatever Jesus calls us to do, it is a privilege to serve.

—What small and seemingly mundane tasks are you doing today?
—How can you see each one of these little jobs as an act of obedience and service to Jesus?
—How do your small actions fit into the bigger picture of what your family, church and community are doing to care for God's world and God's people?

Read Luke 19:35-40:

35 Then they brought it to Jesus; and after throwing their cloaks on the colt, they set Jesus on it. 36 As he rode along, people kept spreading their cloaks on the road. 37 As he was now approaching the path down from the Mount of Olives, the whole multitude of the disciples began to praise God joyfully with a loud voice for all the deeds of power that they had seen, 38 saying,

"Blessed is the king
    who comes in the name of the Lord!
Peace in heaven,
    and glory in the highest heaven!"

39 Some of the Pharisees in the crowd said to him, "Teacher, order your disciples to stop." 40 He answered, "I tell you, if these were silent, the stones would shout out."

Lord, What a Parade!
LYONS 10.10.11.11 ("O Worship the King,
All Glorious Above!")

Lord, what a parade! The crowd quickly grew;
what noise they all made in welcoming you.
"Hosanna!" they shouted. "It's David's own son!
Hosanna! Come save us! God's reign has begun!"

They welcomed you in, a conquering king,
yet what kind of reign would you really bring?
It wasn't a war horse you rode on that day;
a creature of peace carried you on your way.

Did those in that crowd expect something more
than one who reached out in love to the poor?
Did they think a savior with armies was best,
or did they remember: the peaceful are blessed?

Lord Jesus, it's true — we give you glad praise,
yet living for you will challenge our ways.
So may we be open and welcome your reign.
Hosanna! Come save us! Renew us again!

Biblical References: Matthew 21:1-11; Mark 11:1-11; Luke 19:28-40;
John 12:12-19; Zechariah 9:9-10; Matthew 5:9
Tune: Joseph Martin Kraus, 1784; until recently attributed to Johann
Michael Haydn
Text: Copyright © 2011 by Carolyn Winfrey Gillette.
All rights reserved.
Email: carolynshymns@gmail.com
New Hymns: www.carolynshymns.com

Reflection - Lord, What a Parade!

As a pastor, I have served in churches that have had wonderful Palm Sunday processions. In one church, the whole Sunday School marched into the sanctuary, with the children waving palm branches, while everyone sang, "Hosanna, loud hosanna, the little children sang..." On Palm Sundays, many of us try to re-create just a little bit of the excitement that the crowd must have experienced as they welcomed Jesus into the city.

In recent years, our Palm Sunday observances have become Palm-and-Passion Sunday worship services. We move, in worship, from the excitement of the welcoming crowd to the angry cries of the stirred-up crowd.

Quite honestly, there are times we are like some of the people in the crowd. We get disillusioned with Jesus, too. We ask, "If Jesus is Lord, if God is loving, why did that child in my town end up dying?" We wonder, "Jesus talked about forgiveness, and I know I'm supposed to obey, but I just can't forgive." We see others growing disillusioned, too. We hear the news stories of hate-filled, racist, nationalists saying, "We've tried Jesus' way of love and look...we've had enough of it. Now we'll use violence instead." This is what can happen when people get disillusioned with Jesus' way.

Sometimes the disillusionment becomes institutionalized. Some states are moving toward limiting voting rights in order that powerful people might remain in power. Some nations are flexing their military muscles and threatening others out of a search for power and position. We confess that we and others— including others who claim to follow Christ— set our vision on the wrong ways. In the words of the hymn,

"Did they think a savior with armies was best,
or did they remember: the peaceful are blessed?"

Every day as Christians, we face a choice: Will we shout
praises to the humble One who came to serve, riding on a
donkey, or will we shout accusations to the One who didn't
grab power the way we wanted him to? Will we wave a
palm branch or will we wave a sword?

—What does it mean that Jesus rode into the city in
humility?
—What does it mean that he lived his life among the poor?
—Is there some way you can witness to the truth that
Jesus came in peace, to love and to serve, and not to grab
power by using strength?
—Is there some way you, yourself, need to re-affirm Jesus'
way of humble service?

Read Luke 19:45-48:

45 Then he entered the temple and began to drive out those who were selling things there; 46 and he said, "It is written,
'My house shall be a house of prayer';
   but you have made it a den of robbers."

47 Every day he was teaching in the temple. The chief priests, the scribes, and the leaders of the people kept looking for a way to kill him; 48 but they did not find anything they could do, for all the people were spellbound by what they heard.

When Christ Went to the Temple
LLANGLOFFAN 7.6.7.6 D ("Rejoice, Rejoice, Believers")

When Christ went to the Temple
to worship God one day,
He entered through the courtyard
where anyone could pray.
That court was for the nations —
and all could enter in.
But Jesus found a market,
a shameful robbers' den.

There, cattle, sheep and pigeons
were sold for sacrifice,
And moneychangers shouted
of quality and price.
Outsiders could not enter
the inner courts for prayer.
Their only place to worship
was in the courtyard there.

When prayer gave way to profit,
and pride closed many doors,
The Lord cried out in anger
and made a whip of cords.
He shooed the sheep and cattle
and scattered pigeons, too.
God's house was for all people —
not for a chosen few.

O God, you love the nations
and call us all to pray.
Forgive us when our worship
turns other folk away.
As Christ, in loving protest,
fought prejudice and pride,
May we who follow Jesus
now welcome all inside.

Biblical References: Matthew 21:12-17; Mark 11:15-19; Luke 19:45-48;
John 2:13-16
Tune: Traditional Welsh melody, from Daniel Evans' *Hymnau a Thonau*
(*Hymns and Tunes*), 1865

Reflection - When Christ Went to the Temple

John's gospel gives us the story of Jesus' cleansing the Temple as we often see it depicted in artists' paintings— with Jesus brandishing a whip (John 2:15). The NRSV and the NIV Bibles both give us the important detail that Jesus shooed the animals out of the Temple by waving a makeshift whip— probably just a bunch of belts— to get the animals to move along. He did not use this homemade whip on the people.

Luke's gospel gives us some additional insights about this Temple story. After Jesus entered the city, he went to the Temple, where the outer courtyard was the courtyard for the nations. It was the one part of the Temple where the Gentiles, the outsiders, were allowed to go. It was so filled with sellers shouting for people to buy their goods that it was unlikely anyone could pray there.

Did you ever find that your favorite place was taken over by someone for some other purpose? That your favorite "thinking tree" in a park was the place others chose to set up a concession stand? That the corner of your carefully designed Sunday School classroom became the repository for a big pile of church junk? That your online Zoom meeting was disrupted by a Zoom bomber who screen-shared offensive things?

In all of these situations, you might say, "That shows a lack of respect. I don't even have a place where I belong and feel safe anymore!" Jesus saw that the outsiders who wanted to worship God, or at least to learn about God, had been pushed aside. As he swished out the animals, shooing them along as a good Shepherd would do, he said, "'My house shall be a house of prayer'; but you have made it a den of robbers."

It was clear this wasn't a major uprising. Luke tells us that, after this event, Jesus came back to the Temple every day. He kept on teaching the people, and they were amazed by his teaching— about love, and welcome, and welcoming the outsider.

There is a wonderful story of welcome that is part of our family story. When my mother was in the hospital for my birth, she was having serious medical issues; the doctor told my father that my mother might die, and I might die, too. The doctor told Dad (in a time when fathers were not allowed in the delivery room), "Go somewhere for a while and pray, while we take care of your wife and new baby." So he wandered out of the hospital looking for a church building where he could go in and pray. The first church he came to had a locked door. The next church down the street was a Presbyterian church, and the door was open; he went into the sanctuary and prayed for his wife and new daughter. My mother and I both survived, and my United Methodist mother commented to me that that event was the beginning of my becoming Presbyterian! It began with an open door and a welcome place to pray.

—When have you felt "squeezed out" of a special place that you wanted to be?
—When have you been welcomed in by someone who valued you deeply?
—When have you treasured being able to be in a "house of prayer" that let you, the outsider, in?

Chapter 20

Read Luke 20:20-26:

20 So they watched him and sent spies who pretended to be honest, in order to trap him by what he said, so as to hand him over to the jurisdiction and authority of the governor. 21 So they asked him, "Teacher, we know that you are right in what you say and teach, and you show deference to no one, but teach the way of God in accordance with truth. 22 Is it lawful for us to pay taxes to the emperor, or not?" 23 But he perceived their craftiness and said to them, 24 "Show me a denarius. Whose head and whose title does it bear?" They said, "The emperor's." 25 He said to them, "Then give to the emperor the things that are the emperor's, and to God the things that are God's." 26 And they were not able in the presence of the people to trap him by what he said; and being amazed by his answer, they became silent.

Is It Lawful to Pay Taxes?
BEACH SPRING 8.7.8.7 D ("God Whose Giving Knows No Ending")

"Is it lawful to pay taxes
when they prop up Caesar's rule?"
So some people asked of Jesus,
wanting him to seem a fool.
Saying "no" would be sedition;
saying "yes" would be a sin.
Jesus changed the conversation,
calling them to look within.

"Find a tax coin in your treasure;
see the image that it bears.
Give to Caesar what is Caesar's.
(Give to rulers what is theirs.)"
Yet he pressed on with his message;
"Give to God what is God's own."
We who bear our Maker's image
worship God and God alone.

Lord of all, in every nation,
may your word be understood —
That we have an obligation
to support the common good.
May our taxes, all together,
fund our working hand in hand
So that life will be made better
for all people in this land.

Still, we also hear your teaching:
"Give to God what God is due."
May no ruler — overreaching —
try to take the place of you.
May we listen to your message,
may we honor what is yours;
May we, living in your image,
seek your kingdom that endures.

Biblical References: Matthew 22:15-22; Mark 12:13-17; Luke 20:20-26
Tune: *The Sacred Harp*, 1844; attributed to Benjamin Franklin White
Text: Copyright © 2014 by Carolyn Winfrey Gillette.
Email: carolynshymns@gmail.com
New Hymns: www.carolynshymns.com

Reflection - Is It Lawful to Pay Taxes?

This hymn is based on Jesus' teaching of "rendering to Caesar" and "rendering to God."

There's a children's song I learned in Sunday school, "Tell me whose side are you leanin' on? I'm leanin' on the Lord's side!" There's another song that begins, "I have decided to follow Jesus… no turning back… no turning back." These songs challenged me, when I was young, to choose God above all else. They echo the words in Joshua 24:15: "As for me and my house, we will serve the Lord."

One day, some people decided to try to trap Jesus. "Is it lawful to pay taxes to Caesar?" they asked Jesus. They meant for it to be a trick question. No matter how Jesus answered it, he would be in trouble with someone. Jesus answered, "Give to Caesar what belongs to Caesar, and give to God what belongs to God."

There is a place for us, as faithful people, to support the government. This is something that, unfortunately, a lot of people have forgotten. January 6, 2021 was a sad day in the United States, when rioters went into the Capitol Building in an attempt to overthrow a free and fair election. Jesus teaches us that we have an obligation to support the government and to work for the common good. Governments build schools, bridges, and roads; they provide medical care and emergency services. They offer a safety net to people who are poor. They keep our food sources relatively safe. They make laws to protect our drinking water. A good government sees to it that it takes care of the least of these— the very young, the poor, the struggling, the old. A good government works hard to keep its people safe. We as Christians have many reasons to support our government leaders as they work to help citizens and others, too.

Jesus teaches, again and again, that our calling is to be loving. We are loving when we choose to build communities… to lift up those in need… to creatively care for the earth… to live humbly… to show kindness. When we love our neighbors, we are also being loving toward God, and then everything else falls into place. We can give to Caesar what belongs to Caesar, and that's a good thing.

Always, though, our highest loyalty is to God. God created us and we are made in God's image. There is no greater joy than giving to God what belongs to God— our whole lives!

—What are the good things that your taxes do, to provide for the common good?
—What are the ways you can build a stronger local government in your community?
—How do your actions support the rights of every person in this nation?
—Did you ever realize you had to make a choice between supporting your country and following Jesus?   How did Jesus' command to love help you decide what to do?

Read Luke 20:27-38:

27 Some Sadducees, those who say there is no resurrection, came to him 28 and asked him a question, "Teacher, Moses wrote for us that if a man's brother dies, leaving a wife but no children, the man shall marry the widow and raise up children for his brother. 29 Now there were seven brothers; the first married, and died childless; 30 then the second 31 and the third married her, and so in the same way all seven died childless. 32 Finally the woman also died. 33 In the resurrection, therefore, whose wife will the woman be? For the seven had married her."

34 Jesus said to them, "Those who belong to this age marry and are given in marriage; 35 but those who are considered worthy of a place in that age and in the resurrection from the dead neither marry nor are given in marriage. 36 Indeed they cannot die anymore, because they are like angels and are children of God, being children of the resurrection. 37 And the fact that the dead are raised Moses himself showed, in the story about the bush, where he speaks of the Lord as the God of Abraham, the God of Isaac, and the God of Jacob. 38 Now he is God not of the dead, but of the living; for to him all of them are alive."

Some People Who Questioned
ASH GROVE 6.6.11.6.6.11 D ("Let All Things Now Living")

Some people who questioned that there's resurrection
Asked Jesus to tell them of heavenly life.
"The teaching of Moses says our faith supposes
A brother must marry his dead brother's wife."
They said, "It's a sure thing; a man needs some offspring,
So one woman married her dead husband's kin.
'Twas first to one brother, and then to another —
Not one time but many — she married again."

"Not one time, but seven! When she gets to heaven,
Now which brother's wife will that poor widow be?"
So Jesus said clearly the answer's not nearly
The same as the mapping of some family tree.
"In this life folks marry, but those who are worthy
Find heaven is different; they won't marry there.
Like angels in heaven, as God's cherished children,
They'll know of a life that's beyond all compare."

O God, we're still trying to understand dying
And many still wonder if heaven is real.
Yet Christ clearly told us that death cannot hold us;
We'll know of a new life your love will reveal.
Through Jesus, remind us, by your loving kindness,
As Abraham, Isaac and Jacob still live,
When all stand before you, we'll praise and adore you;
And sing with the angels of life that you give!

Biblical References: Matthew 22:24-33; Mark 12:18-27; Luke 20:27-38
Tune: Traditional Welsh melody
Text: Copyright © 2016 by Carolyn Winfrey Gillette.
All rights reserved.
Email: carolynshymns@gmail.com
New Hymns: www.carolynshymns.com

Reflection - Some People Who Questioned

"Some People Who Questioned" is a hymn celebrating Jesus' teaching on heaven. ASH GROVE (the tune commonly used for "Let All Things Now Living") is a wonderful tune for telling a story. I have written several hymns to this lively tune because it allows for a certain playfulness with the language: "The Terrible Sin of the People of Nineveh" (about Jonah), "A King Planned a Party (Jesus' parable about the wedding banquet), "Young Joseph the Dreamer" (about Joseph in the Old Testament) and "When Mary and Joseph Crossed Over the Border" (about the Holy Family fleeing into Egypt), to name a few.

This particular hymn lifts up Jesus' teaching about heaven. Some religious leaders presented Jesus with a riddle: A series of brothers, one at a time, married a certain woman, and one at a time, each brother died. Whose wife will she be in heaven? The ironic part of the story is that these religious leaders didn't even believe in heaven; they simply wanted to catch Jesus in his own words.

The leaders presented this as a riddle; Jesus answered them with the deep understanding of the One who knows God intimately, and who knows the gift of heaven that we long for. Jesus used some Old Testament teachings to make it clear: God is the God of the living, not the dead. Jesus would go on to give his life so that we would have a great and wonderful gift— the gift of life that begins here and now, and that will continue in heaven with God.

When my mother was ill this past fall with Covid, we were not able to see her in person in the final two weeks of her life. She was in the Covid unit at a nursing home where she had gone for rehab after falling and breaking a couple of toes. We did get to talk to her on daily video chats; the nurse lovingly held an iPad for her whenever we wanted to chat. She told me several times in the last year:

"I'm not afraid of dying." She knew Jesus. She knew that, whenever she died, she would be going home.

—When have you experienced the death of a loved one and the grief that comes with such a loss?
—How have the stories of Jesus, including this one, given you hope?
—How has the faithful witness of a friend or family member given you hope?
—How does the promise of heaven change the way you live here and now, on earth?

Chapter 21

Read Luke 21:25-36, including these words:

25 "There will be signs in the sun, the moon, and the stars, and on the earth distress among nations confused by the roaring of the sea and the waves. 26 People will faint from fear and foreboding of what is coming upon the world, for the powers of the heavens will be shaken. 27 Then they will see 'the Son of Man coming in a cloud' with power and great glory. 28 Now when these things begin to take place, stand up and raise your heads, because your redemption is drawing near."

29 Then he told them a parable: "Look at the fig tree…"
(Luke 21:25-29)

God's World Is Changing
BUNESSAN 5.5.5.4 D ("Morning Has Broken")

God's world is changing; where is it going?
Nations are raging; look at their fear!
Many are anxious, filled with foreboding;
We wait in faith, for God's reign is near.

"Look at the fig tree!" See what it's doing.
Look at the signs in heaven above.
God is at work here, building, renewing;
Some are afraid, but we know God's love.

This world is drifting, filled with distraction!
Many are wandering; some fall away.
We wait in faith! We're ready for action.
We're on our guard to greet God's new day.

What should we do, Lord, while we are waiting?
Some just sit back while troubles increase.
Others respond by fighting and hating.
We hear your call to work for your peace.

Lord, may we use each day that we're given —
Helping the hungry, homeless and poor.
Then we'll be ready for what you're bringing
When Christ will come and reign evermore.

Biblical References: Psalm 25:5-10; Luke 21:25-36; Matthew 25:31-46
Tune: Traditional Gaelic melody
Text: Copyright © 2015 by Carolyn Winfrey Gillette.
All rights reserved.
Email: carolynshymns@gmail.com
New Hymns: www.carolynshymns.com

Reflection - God's World is Changing

"God's World Is Changing…Nations are raging! Look at their fear." This line, from the hymn, "God's World Is Changing" reminds us that change so often leads to worry. Jesus was describing a world in turmoil: "People will faint from fear and foreboding of what is coming upon the world, for the powers of the heavens will be shaken." We do not pretend to understand the future; even Jesus himself said that no one knows the future, not even the Son of Man.

Yet, we do know fear. It's hard to turn to the news without finding reasons to be upset. Climate change, the aggressiveness and violence of nations, long lines of refugees, drug overdose rates, and the pandemic are all upsetting to us.

Jesus said, "Look at the fig tree." Look at the seasons. You can tell when they are changing. Look at the world. The changes should lead us to keep alert and to pay attention to the future so we can make decisions about how to live in the present. Jesus' call to us in the present is simply to be faithful and loving on each day we are given. "Be on guard" means to be alert to each day's opportunities to serve, no matter what life brings.

Sometimes the upheavals we face aren't global or national. In June of 2019, my husband Bruce and I were in the Emergency Room in a-small town hospital near our home when we learned the news that Bruce had acute leukemia. He was taken by ambulance to a big teaching hospital three hours away. Months later, he had a bone marrow transplant. Ever since that time, he has been recovering from his illness and transplant, and he has been dealing with a suppressed immune system during the pandemic. Finally, finally, his health is improving.

There was no way for us to see that coming. It was as if the foundations of our everyday lives were shaken. Since that time, we have learned to celebrate the gift of each new day. Bruce is a pastor, and when he was in the hospital, on the days when he was feeling well enough, he would find opportunities to listen to staff members who were stressed about life issues, family problems and work challenges. He would encourage other patients when the passed them in the hallways. One night, he prayed with the family of a patient who had died in the hospital room next door.

In the words of the hymn,

"Lord, may we use each day that we're given —
Helping the hungry, homeless and poor.
Then we'll be ready for what you're bringing
When Christ will come and reign evermore."

—What causes you fear as you look around at our world?
—What causes you fear as you look at your personal and family life?
—When you are facing a crisis, it is important to care for your own needs. At the same time, a personal crisis for you can sometimes be an opportunity to reach out to someone else. When did you reach out to someone else when you were in crisis— and so find you were welcoming Jesus?

Chapter 22

Read Luke 22:39-53, including these words:

39 He came out and went, as was his custom, to the Mount of Olives; and the disciples followed him. 40 When he reached the place, he said to them, "Pray that you may not come into the time of trial." 41 Then he withdrew from them about a stone's throw, knelt down, and prayed, 42 "Father, if you are willing, remove this cup from me; yet, not my will but yours be done." (Luke 22:39-46)

Jesus Went Out to a Garden
BEACH SPRING 8.7.8.7 D ("God Whose Giving Knows No Ending")

Jesus went out to a garden
to a quiet place to pray.
In the night, a crowd came round him,
led by Judas on their way.
They seized Jesus to arrest him;
someone near then drew a sword.
Soon a slave was injured, suffering
there beside our suffering Lord.

Jesus spoke to stop the violence:
"Put your sword back in its place."
Then he touched the slave and healed him
In a moment filled with grace.
For as violence leads to violence
causing more distress and pain —
So compassion in abundance
Is a witness to God's reign.

God of love, we pause and wonder:
Did that slave give quiet praise?
Yet the story marches onward
with the pain that it portrays.
For the One who brought such healing
soon was broken, on a cross,
To our sinful world revealing
violence has an awful cost.

God, the gospels bear a witness:
Your Son's death was not the end.
By your grace, you raised up Jesus;
Sin and violence did not win.
May we work to end all suffering;
lead us in Christ's peaceful way.
May his peace become an offering
that we share throughout each day

Biblical References: Matthew 26:47-56; Mark 14:43-50;
Luke 22:47-53; John 18:1-11
Tune: *The Sacred Harp*, 1844; attributed to Benjamin Franklin White
Text: Copyright © 2012 by Carolyn Winfrey Gillette.
All rights reserved.
Email: carolynshymns@gmail.com
New Hymns: www.carolynshymns.com

Reflection - Jesus Went Out to a Garden

This hymn recalls Jesus' time of prayer on the Mount of Olives and his arrest in the garden.

One of the details in this story is how quick one of the disciples was, to draw a sword in Jesus' defense. Jesus was facing the anguish of knowing what lay ahead for him. The disciples were surely terrified. So often violence comes out of our intense fear of things that we cannot control. The response of the disciples was to ask, "Lord, should we strike with the sword?"

I am reminded of the many times we have seen Christians strike with the sword— sometimes in ways violent enough to cut off someone's ear or worse— in the name of Jesus. During the Civil Rights Movement, countless people bearing the name of Christ turned fire hoses and police dogs on Black citizens and their allies. More recently, people calling themselves Christians, working for the government, ripped immigrant children out of the hands of their mothers and took them away, placing them in foster homes and to a large extent losing them in the foster care system. People carrying signs saying they love Jesus were among those who recently broke into the Capitol building and rioted, injuring and killing people along the way. Many of the people who did these things probably went to church the next Sunday. Some of them probably stood in their churches and sang songs about Jesus' love. Many of them, mistakenly, thought they were defending God.

All of them were wrong. First, their causes were hate-filled, not loving, ones. Second, people who do these things are wrong because they somehow think they are defending Jesus. Jesus does not need for us to defend him. He is Lord. His way is the way of love. Jesus calls us to train ourselves to react, impulsively, with love and not with violence. I imagine there are many times that Jesus looks at our violent actions and reactions, done out of fear or impulse or hatred, and says, "No more of this!" So we have our calling, and it is one that Jesus made clear especially at this stressful time toward the end of his earthly life:

"May we work to end all suffering;
lead us in Christ's peaceful way.
May his peace become an offering
that we share throughout each day."

—When have you used violence? Are there times you believe it is necessary?
—What do Jesus' words teach us about seeking the most peaceful way?
—Does it take more creativity and wisdom to live peacefully than to react with anger and violence?
—How can you help people who have experienced violence and abuse— so they will know peace, justice and safety?

Read Luke 22:54-62, including these words:

54 Then they seized him and led him away, bringing him into the high priest's house. But Peter was following at a distance. 55 When they had kindled a fire in the middle of the courtyard and sat down together, Peter sat among them. 56 Then a servant-girl, seeing him in the firelight, stared at him and said, "This man also was with him." 57 But he denied it, saying, "Woman, I do not know him..." (Luke 22:54-57)

As Peter Stood Outside in Fear

O WALY WALY 8.8.8.8 ("Though I May Speak")

As Peter stood outside in fear,
A woman said, "I've seen you here.
You were with him! Just say it's so!"
But three times, Peter answered, "No!"

Why is it, Lord, that when we're stressed
We feel things more and think things less?
We let the fear that is inside
Become our ruler and our guide.

We're called to welcome strangers in
Yet we let fear and hatred win.
When we ignore what's just and true,
O Lord, are we denying you?

We say the things we ought not say;
We let concerns control the day.
Lord, take our fear and in its place,
Fill us with love and hope and grace.

In anxious times, Lord, make us wise
To look within our inner lives.
When fear tempts us to cave to sin,
May we seek truth and let love win!

Biblical References: Mark 14:66-72; Matthew 26:69-75;
Luke 22:54-62; John 18:15-18; John 25-27; Proverbs 29:25;
1 John 4:16-21
Tune: Traditional English melody
Text: Copyright © 2018 by Carolyn Winfrey Gillette.
All rights reserved.
Email: carolynshymns@gmail.com
New Hymns: www.carolynshymns.com

Reflection - As Peter Stood Outside in Fear

The fear in the Passion story continues in this biblical reading and hymn about Peter denying Jesus. Again, we see how fear causes us to do things we probably wouldn't do otherwise. Our brains go into survival mode. In the words of the hymn,

"Why is it, Lord, that when we're stressed
We feel things more and think things less?
We let the fear that is inside
Become our ruler and our guide."

We can imagine Peter standing there, off in the shadows, trying to be invisible, then having a local woman call attention to him: "Look! He's one of them! He was with Jesus!" His impulsive reaction was to deny ever having known Jesus.

Have you ever wanted to be invisible? You knew the right thing to do— the ethical thing. Yet you wanted to stay in the background, not making a scene, not having to 'fess up to which side of a disagreement you were taking. Maybe you saw trouble on the subway, and you moved to a different subway car or stared out the window. Or maybe you saw someone being harassed in a store and you looked away. Or you heard someone in a Sunday school class saying prejudiced things about immigrants or some oppressed minority and you knew what to do— but you were tired, and you just wanted the uncomfortable conversation to go away, so you said nothing.

There will come times in all of our lives when we are called to strongly and boldly affirm what we believe, even at great risk to ourselves. An employee of a large corporation once told me that her company routinely broke pollution laws. It was accepted practice.

The company executives believed that it was cheaper to pay the fines than to use ethical, clean standards for making their product. The woman was caught standing in a corner, so to speak, wanting to be invisible. If she spoke the truth about the company's polluting decisions, they might say, "You're one of them! You're not loyal to us!"

Should she state her belief that the company wrong? Should she stand up and say, "Look at me! This is who I stand with. This is what I believe in."? Or should she melt into the background by the fire like Peter (or by the water cooler in the office) and be quiet? In the words of the hymn,

"When we ignore what's just and true,
O Lord, are we denying you?"

—When were you confronted for loving God, loving neighbor, or loving God's creation? Did someone accuse you of being unpatriotic? Of not "protecting our way of life"? Of not having a good head for business? Of loving and caring for the wrong people?
—What was your answer?

Read Luke 22:63-71, including these words:

66 When day came, the assembly of the elders of the people, both chief priests and scribes, gathered together, and they brought him to their council. 67 They said, "If you are the Messiah, tell us." He replied, "If I tell you, you will not believe; 68 and if I question you, you will not answer. 69 But from now on the Son of Man will be seated at the right hand of the power of God." 70 All of them asked, "Are you, then, the Son of God?" He said to them, "You say that I am." 71 Then they said, "What further testimony do we need? We have heard it ourselves from his own lips!" (Luke 22:66-71)

As Jesus Faced the Council

ST. CHRISTOPHER 7.6.8.6.8.6.8.6 ("Beneath the Cross of Jesus")

As Jesus faced the council,
the accusations flew,
Till someone turned and said to him,
"Now tell us, who are you?
Are you the Christ, God's chosen one?"
He answered them: "I am —
And soon the Son of Man will reign
in power, at God's right hand."

Nearby, out in the courtyard,
next to the fire's warm glow,
The Rock named Peter sat, afraid,
not sure where he should go.
He longed for news about the Lord,
and so he stayed close by,
But when they asked him who he was,
he chose to tell a lie.

A servant said, "You're with him!
I saw you two before."
Yet once and twice and still again,
the Rock denied his Lord.
He said, "I do not understand!"
He firmly answered, "No!"
He claimed, "I do not know that man,"
and then the rooster crowed.

O Christ, we are like Peter,
for we deny you, too.
Concerned for what the world might say,
we do not live for you.
May we (like Peter later on)
have courage to proclaim:
"We're bound to Christ. He is our Lord!
We'll follow in his name!"

Biblical References: Matthew 26:57-75; Mark 14:53-72;
Luke 22:54-71; John 18:15-27; Acts 2:14-40
Tune: Frederick Charles Maker, 1881
Text: Copyright © 2015 by Carolyn Winfrey Gillette.
All rights reserved.
Email: carolynshymns@gmail.com
New Hymns: www.carolynshymns.com

Reflection - As Jesus Faced the Council

We are grateful to United Methodist Bishop Peggy Johnson for suggesting that a hymn be written on the biblical story of Jesus appearing before the Council. In this part of the Passion story, we see Jesus being questioned by the religious leaders. We see Jesus responding steadily, faithfully, and truthfully.

I am grateful for Jesus' steadiness in the face of evil. I know how difficult it can be to stay strong. I remember going into the courtroom when we had our foster son. There were things we needed to say— things the court needed to hear. It can be hard to speak the truth in places where others hold such power and where angry things are being said. Looking back, I wonder if there were things I could have said, or things I could have done differently, to speak the truth in a setting that was determining a child's future.

I thank God that, as Jesus faced the Council, he spoke with truth and love, with wisdom and courage. I pray that in the times I need to speak out, God will help me do the same.

—When have you been brave to speak the truth in a difficult, adversarial situation?
—When have you tried to blend into the background like Peter did?
—What have these experiences in your life taught you, over time, about God's forgiveness?

Chapter 23

Read Luke 23:33-34:

33 When they came to the place that is called The Skull, they crucified Jesus there with the criminals, one on his right and one on his left. [34 Then Jesus said, "Father, forgive them; for they do not know what they are doing."] And they cast lots to divide his clothing.

Read also Luke 23:39-43:

39 One of the criminals who were hanged there kept deriding him and saying, "Are you not the Messiah? Save yourself and us!" 40 But the other rebuked him, saying, "Do you not fear God, since you are under the same sentence of condemnation? 41 And we indeed have been condemned justly, for we are getting what we deserve for our deeds, but this man has done nothing wrong." 42 Then he said, "Jesus, remember me when you come into your kingdom." 43 He replied, "Truly I tell you, today you will be with me in Paradise."

Read also Luke 23:46:

46 Then Jesus, crying with a loud voice, said, "Father, into your hands I commend my spirit." Having said this, he breathed his last.

Father, Forgive Them
ADELAIDE 5.4.5.4 D ("Have Thine Own Way, Lord")

"Father, forgive them!" Jesus, you prayed;
Even at death, your love was profound.
You were rejected, you were betrayed —
Yet in your word here, mercies abound.

Two hung beside you, dying in pain;
One saw, in faith, your love's sacrifice.
You told that man who called on your name,
"You will be with me in Paradise."

"This is your mother... This is your son."
You blessed the life your loved ones would share.
So in your church, you give to each one
Love's healing bonds — an answer to prayer.

You prayed a Psalm that everyone knew:
"Why have you left me here all alone?"
Did you recall that Psalm's ending, too? —
God will deliver! Let it be known!

You cried, "I'm thirsty!" suffering Lord.
Who would give comfort? What would they do?
Teach us again: When we serve the poor,
We too are giving water to you.

"It is completed!" All was fulfilled.
You had been faithful, living God's way.
You knew the truth: Love could not be killed;
There would be triumph on the third day.

"Father!" You cried out, praying to God,
"Into your hands my spirit I give."
Then on the cross, as love's final Word,
You died so all God's children might live.

Biblical References: Luke 23:33-34, 39-43, 46; John 19:25-29;
Mark 15:33-34
Tune: George Coles Stebbins, 1907
Email: carolynshymns@gmail.com
New Hymns: www.carolynshymns.com

Reflection - Father, Forgive Them

This hymn is inspired by Jesus' Seven Last Words from the Cross. Three of them are found in Luke's Gospel:

There is the word of Reconciliation: "Father, forgive them; for they do not know what they are doing." Jesus took away the barriers between our sinful selves and God.

There is the word of Habitation and Hope: To the thief on the cross next to him, Jesus said, "Truly I tell you, today you will be with me in Paradise." The sinner heard the promise of a new place to live— a wonderful place, in the presence of Jesus.

And finally, there was the word of Commendation: "Father, into your hands I commend my spirit."

All three of these words are so important to the Gospel message of Jesus. In the times we have fallen short, we need forgiveness and an opportunity to begin again. In the times we feel alone and scared, we need the promise that Jesus will always be with us and we will be with Jesus. In the times we think we don't need anybody, we need to remember, as Jesus did, that our lives are in God's hands.

Then, we need to share these gifts with others— by forgiving our enemies, welcoming people who are on the outside, and by helping others know they are in the loving embrace of God.

—Which word of Jesus from the cross speaks to you today?

Chapter 24

Read Luke 24:1-5:

1 But on the first day of the week, at early dawn, they came to the tomb, taking the spices that they had prepared. ² They found the stone rolled away from the tomb, ³ but when they went in, they did not find the body. ⁴ While they were perplexed about this, suddenly two men in dazzling clothes stood beside them. ⁵ The women were terrified and bowed their faces to the ground, but the men said to them, "Why do you look for the living among the dead? He is not here, but has risen.

Come and Join the Celebration
NETTLETON 8.7.8.7 D ("Come, Thou Fount of Every Blessing")

Come and join the celebration!
Praise the Lord and gladly sing.
Hear the gospel proclamation:
God in Christ changed everything!
Tell again the wondrous story;
let your praises rise above.
God, we sing and give you glory
for your everlasting love.

Sing with joy, for on a Sunday
friends of Jesus went to grieve.
Soon they found his tomb was empty;
telling others, they believed.
God of miracle and wonder,
Jesus died and lives again.
Death has lost, for you are stronger;
all creation sings, "Amen!"

God, we sing, for there is nothing
that can keep your love away —
Not oppression, hardship, famine,
things to come or things today.
Heights and depths cannot defeat us;
death will never be the same.
Christ is risen! So you promise:
we have life in Jesus' name.

Sing with joy, each generation!
Sing with those who've gone before.
Join the kingdom celebration,
old and young, both rich and poor.
We have life, for we're forgiven;
where, O death, is now your sting?
Born of dust, we're claimed for heaven,
so let all God's people sing.

Biblical References: Genesis 2:7; Luke 24:1-12; Romans 8:26-39;
1 Corinthians 15; Philippians 2:9-11
Tune: John Wyeth's *Repository of Sacred Music*, 1813
Alternate tune: ANN'S TUNE, Hal Hopson, copyright 2010 Hope
Publishing Company
Text: Copyright © 2010 by Carolyn Winfrey Gillette.
All rights reserved.
Email: carolynshymns@gmail.com
New Hymns: www.carolynshymns.com

Reflection - Come and Join the Celebration

Finally, we celebrate Easter! This hymn was commissioned by Grace Covenant Presbyterian Church in memory and honor of Ann Gettys Nash; it was sung for the first time in their worship service on April 18, 2010 in Asheville, North Carolina. The gifted composer Hal Hopson wrote new music for this hymn titled "Ann's Tune." It can also be sung to a variety of 8.7.8.7.D meter hymns, including NETTLETON ("Come, Thou Fount of Every Blessing")

The Easter story is the basis for our faith as Christians. God raised Jesus from the dead and showed us that he has conquered death. You and I are often caught up in the problems of the world. Especially during the pandemic, we have watched loved ones suffer. During the war in Ukraine, we have watched violence spiral out of control. We have been surrounded by death and by people hurting in countless ways. Yet in the words of the hymn,

"God, we sing, for there is nothing
that can keep your love away —
Not oppression, hardship, famine,
things to come or things today.
Heights and depths cannot defeat us;
death will never be the same.
Christ is risen! So you promise:
we have life in Jesus' name."

With my mother's death a few months ago from Covid, Bruce and I have now lost all four of our parents. As pastors, we have officiated at countless funerals— for children and old people and those in-between, for dedicated Sunday school teachers and for people who kept pretty quiet about their faith. We have buried plenty of saints and sinners— and quite honestly, most people are a mix of the two. We know the time will come when we will see our loved ones, God's beloved children, again:

"Sing with joy, each generation!
Sing with those who've gone before.
Join the kingdom celebration,
old and young, both rich and poor."

We sing our faith, out loud or in the quietness of our hearts, because "born of dust, we're claimed for heaven."

That doesn't mean we just sit around waiting for some future time. I remember how Presbyterian minister Fred Rogers, on *Mister Rogers' Neighborhood*, used to sing a song, "Let's think of something to do while we're waiting…" As followers of Jesus' way of love, there's plenty for us to do. In response to Christ's resurrection, I have hymns to write. I have church friends to comfort during a pandemic — even if it's only by phone or standing in their front yard talking to them across the lawn. I have family and friends to care for— even if it means reading stories and chatting with them on Zoom or other ways online. I have grand-children to babysit for— I hope, soon! I have fruit and bread to deliver to a hurting friend.

In response to Christ's resurrection promise of new life, I have a letter to write to the President about immigration reform… a house to make more energy efficient… a compost pile to tend to… a garden to grow…a foreign language to learn so I can help my church resettle a refugee family more easily. In the words of the hymn,

"We have life in Jesus' name."

God calls us to share that life with others— day by day, step by step, one moment of welcome after another.

—What does the resurrection promise have to do with how you will live your life this particular day?
—What will you do differently today, because God in Jesus offers us new life?

Read Luke 24:5-12, including these words:

5 The women were terrified and bowed their faces to the ground, but the men said to them, "Why do you look for the living among the dead? He is not here, but has risen. 6 Remember how he told you, while he was still in Galilee, 7 that the Son of Man must be handed over to sinners, and be crucified, and on the third day rise again." 8 Then they remembered his words, 9 and returning from the tomb, they told all this to the eleven and to all the rest. 10 Now it was Mary Magdalene, Joanna, Mary the mother of James, and the other women with them who told this to the apostles… (Luke 24:5-10)

You Give Us Hope This Easter Day

O WALY WALY 8.8.8.8 ("Though I May Speak")

You give us hope this Easter Day:
O God, in Christ, you make us new!
As we've been blessed, O Lord, we pray,
May these our gifts bless others, too.

When people flee from drought or storm,
When children cry, in need of bread —
May these our gifts keep victims warm
And see that hungry ones are fed.

When workers suffer, long-oppressed,
When neighbors seek to organize,
When those abused weep in distress —
May these our gifts change people's lives.

When churches seek to tend the earth,
When gardens grow on urban lands —
May these our gifts provide new birth,
Clear-flowing waters, helping hands.

O gracious God, you give us life!
This gift is one we're called to share.
May we now serve the risen Christ
Through these our gifts of love and care.

Biblical References: John 20:1-18; Luke 24:1-12
Tune: Traditional English melody
Text: Copyright © 2013 by Carolyn Winfrey Gillette.
All rights reserved.
Email: carolynshymns@gmail.com
New Hymns: www.carolynshymns.com

Reflection - You Give Us Hope This Easter Day

Every year for many years, the Presbyterian Church (USA) has received four special offerings; one of them (usually received during Lent) is the One Great Hour of Sharing Offering that we participate in with other churches. The offering supports efforts to relieve hunger through the Presbyterian Hunger Program, it promotes justice and positive change through the Presbyterian Committee on the Self-Development of People, and it assists many hurting people disaster through Presbyterian Disaster Assistance.

It is appropriate that we receive this offering during Lent and at Easter. Lent is a time when we focus on God's love in Jesus Christ. Jesus told us to love and care for people who are poor, those who are broken-hearted, those who are captive and in trouble, and those who are hurting. At Easter, we celebrate that God is a life-giving God who wants health and wholeness for everyone. What better way is there to thank God for loving us than to pass on God's love to others in need?

Hope is an amazing gift. It is a light-at-the-end-of-the-tunnel gift. It's a new-dawn-breaking gift. It's a food-is-on-the-table-again gift. It's a help-is-on-the-way gift. It's a finally-there-will-be-justice gift.

Recently we have been working with several churches in the area that are actively resettling immigrant and refugee families. Imagine the change from despair to hope that happens— when a family goes from struggling on their own to having people of faith partner with them on their journey. Imagine the feeling that comes when someone says, 'We're neighbors, together. We'll work on this challenge together."

That's what our One Great Hour of Sharing offering helps us to do. It helps our church to say: "We're neighbors, together. We'll work on this challenge together."

—What hope does Easter bring to you?
—What is one thing you can do today, to bring the hope of Easter to a neighbor?

Read Luke 24:28-35, including these words:

28 As they came near the village to which they were going, he walked ahead as if he were going on. 29 But they urged him strongly, saying, "Stay with us, because it is almost evening and the day is now nearly over." So he went in to stay with them. 30 When he was at the table with them, he took bread, blessed and broke it, and gave it to them. 31 Then their eyes were opened, and they recognized him; and he vanished from their sight. (Luke 24:28-31)

God, We Sense Your Peace and Power (Taste)
NETTLETON 8.7.8.7 D ("Come, Thou Fount of Every Blessing")

God, we sense your peace and power
In this place we love so much.
We are moved by gentle fragrance;
We are blessed by healing touch.

In these pews we hear the gospel;
We see life beyond compare.
Here we gather at your table,
Tasting love in meals we share.

Some were walking to Emmaus
Who were grieving, sad and lost.
For they'd loved and cared for Jesus,
And he'd died upon a cross.

Jesus, risen, came and met them;
Soon he served them wine and bread.
Then their grieving was forgotten;
Wonder filled their lives instead.

God of love, we taste your bounty
At the table you prepare.
Here we find there's food a-plenty
That we're called to eat and share.

There is bread and cup for feasting,
There is food for rich and poor;
May we taste your love and blessing
Now, and — yes — forevermore!

Biblical Reference: Luke 24
Tune: John Wyeth's *Repository of Sacred Music*, 1813
Email: carolynshymns@gmail.com
New Hymns: www.carolynshymns.com

Reflection - God, We Sense Your Peace and Power

This hymn was commissioned by Pastor Jeff Gibelius and the Second Presbyterian Church in Carlisle, Pennsylvania, for a Lenten worship/sermon series in 2017 on "Experiencing God Through the Five Senses." The hymn is one of a series of five hymns — all with the same first verse that serves as an introduction. All are available on my website: www.carolynshymns.com For each hymn in the series, after that first verse, there is a second verse based on one of the five senses and the scripture reading for the day. Then, there is a third verse that celebrates the ways we use that sense to experience God in our contemporary lives.

The sense of taste brings back so many memories in us. My mother used to make and freeze homemade applesauce every fall, because there were apple orchards all around her home in Western Maryland. Whenever we went to visit her, she would pull a container of her applesauce out of the freezer, thaw it, and serve it with dinner.

Down in the freezer of the family house, there are still a few containers of her applesauce. When I go to visit my brother there, and when we go to the freezer and get out one of her homemade applesauce containers, I remember my mother— not only making the applesauce, but serving it with love. I remember her carrying it to the table in a serving bowl, filling our stomachs with food, and filling our hearts with old family stories as we shared dinner and dessert.

When Jesus broke the bread at the table, it's no wonder his disciples finally recognized him in the breaking of the bread, in the words he shared, maybe in the stories he told them there at the table. When we share the Lord's

Supper, it is more than a good memory. It is a meal where Christ is present with us in a unique and wonderful way— where, in the words of the hymn,

"Here we taste God's love and blessing,
now and — yes— forevermore."

—What foods bring back strong memories and help you feel present with someone you love?
—When have you been at tables that were particularly "welcome tables"?
—What have been your experiences of sharing the Lord's Supper in church?

Read Luke 24:36-49, including these words:

36 While they were talking about this, Jesus himself stood among them and said to them, "Peace be with you."
37 They were startled and terrified, and thought that they were seeing a ghost. 38 He said to them, "Why are you frightened, and why do doubts arise in your hearts?
39 Look at my hands and my feet; see that it is I myself. Touch me and see; for a ghost does not have flesh and bones as you see that I have." 40 And when he had said this, he showed them his hands and his feet. 41 While in their joy they were disbelieving and still wondering, he said to them, "Have you anything here to eat?" 42 They gave him a piece of broiled fish, 43 and he took it and ate in their presence... (Luke 24:36-43)

O Christ, Your Friends Were Gathered
AURELIA 7.6.7.6 D ("The Church's One Foundation")

O Christ, your friends were gathered
together in a room.
They'd heard the women's stories
about your empty tomb.
Some talked about Emmaus—
they'd seen you breaking bread.
Some claimed that you were risen;
some thought you still were dead.

You met your friends and showed them
your wounded hands and side,
For you were Jesus risen
and Jesus crucified.
You showed them God had triumphed
and God had suffered pain.
And in that intersection,
you made them whole again.

You meet us in the places
where all seems doomed or lost—
Where people face oppression,
where children pay the cost,
Where poor ones cry in hunger,
where illness takes its toll:
You meet us, suffering Savior,
and make the wounded whole.

O Christ, your resurrection
gives hope and life anew.
And yet your wounds and anguish
give peace and promise, too.
For you've been there before us!
Now send us out to be
A church that bears your suffering
and claims your victory.

Biblical References: Luke 24:1-49; Romans 6:4;
Romans 8:17; 2 Corinthians 1:5
Tune: Samuel Sebastian Wesley, 1864
Email: carolynshymns@gmail.com
New Hymns: www.carolynshymns.com

Reflection - O Christ, Your Friends Were Gathered

On Easter, Jesus rose from the dead. On Easter, we celebrate that Jesus appears to us in the dead, dying and despairing places of our lives, and he bring hope and healing and Hallelujahs! Jesus brings new life. In the words of this hymn,

"You meet us in the places
where all seems doomed or lost—
Where people face oppression,
where children pay the cost..."

When I wrote this hymn, I was thinking about how— whenever people are oppressed— it is the children who suffer the most. Look at the latest war we are facing. See the pictures of schools and maternity hospitals that have been bombed. Look at the artwork that children have been drawing in places where there is fighting and war. Look at the pain they draw into their pictures. Today, I saw a video clip of a little girl in a bomb shelter in a subway in Ukraine, singing a Disney song, "Let It Go," for the people around her.   Here was a child who loved Disney movies having to deal with the atrocities of war.

Children do pay the cost for the sin and brokenness in our world. I included a special prayer for them in this hymn. Christ meets the children and families who are hurting so much. My prayer is that we can be the bearers of Christ's wholeness and healing to God's little ones.

Sometimes, in the times and places of great suffering, we see Jesus most clearly. Recent news reports showed three generations of Christians, including an old man, a middle aged woman, and a small child, at a worship service in a bomb shelter in Ukraine. With missiles and bombs coming close to them, they gathered on a Sunday to light candles and to sing the songs of faith.

Jesus met them there.

Jesus meets us in our suffering. With his wounds visible, he reminds us that he knows our suffering because he suffered, too. With his resurrection body, he promises that death does not have the final word. The final word is a word of God's love.

—How, in your community, do children pay the cost of the sins of their parents, grandparents, or people with power and privilege?

—What thing, even a small thing, have you done to bring healing to someone who is broken?

—What thing, even a small thing, have you done to bring healing to a child in your community?

—What letter can your write, or what phone call can you make, to your leaders in Congress today, advocating for the needs of children?

Read Luke 24:48:

48 You are witnesses of these things.

O God, In Christ You Call Us
AURELIA 7.6.7.6 D ("The Church's One Foundation")

O God, in Christ you call us
to witness to your grace —
To share the life you give us
in every time and place.
So many things divide us —
yet we are not our own;
For we belong to Jesus
who prayed, "May they be one."

In Christ is our salvation;
in him you've set us free —
We make this proclamation
in bold humility.
Your image is in others
who follow different ways;
Together, seeking justice,
we offer you our praise.

In Christ, we're bound together;
in him we find your peace.
Yet even as we gather,
the wounds of war increase.
Where terror brings division,
God, make us brave to say
Our churches share a vision
of Jesus' peaceful way.

In Christ, the poor and hungry
are shown they matter, too —
And where your church has plenty,
you give us work to do.
Now may we put in practice
the faith that we declare,
Seek economic justice,
and find new ways to share.

In Christ, you bless creation
and show this planet's worth;
May every congregation
find ways to tend the earth.
Now fill us with your Spirit,
that we, as one, may be
A faithful, loving witness
to all humanity.

Biblical References: Luke 24:48; John 17:21; Luke 10:36-37;
Matthew 5:9; Luke 4:16-19; John 3:16.
Tune: Samuel Sebastian Wesley, 1864
Text: Copyright © 2010 by Carolyn Winfrey Gillette.
 All rights reserved.
Email: carolynshymns@gmail.com
New Hymns: www.carolynshymns.com

Reflection - O God, In Christ You Call Us

This hymn was originally commissioned for the Centennial Ecumenical Gathering and General Assembly of the National Council of Churches of Christ in the USA and Church World Service meeting November 9-11, 2010 in New Orleans. The theme of the assembly was "Witnesses of These Things: Ecumenical Engagement in a New Era." We are witnesses to the Risen Christ. God calls us to live differently because of Easter. God calls us to speak differently because of Easter. God calls us to work with other churches so that our witness to the community is stronger.

In a divided, angry world, God calls us to witness to the unity we have in Christ. In a self-serving world, God calls us to be humble. In an unjust world, God calls us to work for laws that are fair and just. In a violent world, God calls us to follow Christ's way of peace and gentleness. In a hungry world, God calls us to share our bread and make the table wider and longer so everyone has a place. In a world where climate change threatens us all, God calls us to care for God's wonderful, intricate creation— more than we care for profit.

—When have you lived differently this week, because of Jesus?
—When have you taken a risk to be a witness to God's love?
— How is your church partnering with other churches in your community to share God's love?

Read Luke 24:50-53:

[50] Then he led them out as far as Bethany, and, lifting up his hands, he blessed them. [51] While he was blessing them, he withdrew from them and was carried up into heaven. [52] And they worshiped him, and returned to Jerusalem with great joy; [53] and they were continually in the temple blessing God.

O Christ, When You Ascended
LANCASHIRE 7.6.7.6 D ("The Day of Resurrection")

O Christ, when you ascended,
you took your rightful throne;
Your time on earth had ended —
yet we weren't left alone.
You reign o'er earth and heaven;
your Spirit guides our way.
Your prayers uphold your people;
you lead your church each day.

We look at earthly rulers
and see what they command:
We note their years of power,
the borders of their land.
Yet, Lord, you are not bounded
by things like time and space;
Your reign is never-ending,
you rule in every place.

We're tempted. Lord, to leave you
in stories nicely told;
Sometimes we don't believe you
and say your ways are old.
Sometimes we feel so lonely
and live in doubt and fear —
But your ascension means, Lord,
you're present with us here.

It's often quite a challenge
to follow in your Way;
We're easily distracted!
It's hard, Lord, to obey.
Sometimes we give you Sundays —
an hour, maybe two —
But your ascension means, Lord,
all life belongs to you.

One day, O Lord, we'll know you,
as we are fully known;
One day this world of sinners
will bow before your throne.
One day, God's whole creation
will sing and praise your name;
On earth as now in heaven,
we'll celebrate your reign.

Biblical Reference: Luke 24:50-53; Acts 1:1-11
Tune: Henry Thomas Smart, 1835
Text: Copyright © 2007 by Carolyn Winfrey Gillette. All rights reserved.
Copied from *Songs of Grace: New Hymns for God and Neighbor* by
Carolyn Winfrey Gillette (Upper Room Books, 2009).
Email: carolynshymns@gmail.com
New Hymns: www.carolynshymns.com

Reflection - O Christ, When You Ascended

Many of us tend to picture the Ascension of Jesus by imagining Jesus going "up, up and away." Yet the Ascension is more than a story of Jesus leaving earth. It is an affirmation that Jesus is Lord, and it is a story of how we are to live on this earth.

The Ascension is an affirmation that Jesus is praying for us. It is a promise that Jesus is not bound by time and space; there are no boundaries in Christ's reign. It means Jesus is Lord of Sunday, Monday, Tuesday, Wednesday, Thursday, Friday, Saturday. Jesus is Lord of those moments that feel timeless as well— the moments of opportunity, the times of crisis, the new births, the moments of death, the times of despair, the times of hope.

Have you ever felt as if you were "on your own" in a moment of struggle? That you were not sure of Christ's presence? That it didn't matter if you turned away from Jesus' teaching— just a little bit? The Ascension speaks to us in all of these times, reminding us that Jesus' love is like an umbrella of love over every part of our lives and world. It is sometimes a hidden promise, now— but one day it will be clear to everyone:

"One day, God's whole creation
will sing and praise your name;
On earth as now in heaven,
we'll celebrate your reign."

—Have you ever experienced a time when someone you loved was absent from you— traveling, or in the hospital, for example— and at the same time the person was very present to you— in thought, in prayer, or in your decision-making?

—How does Christ's reign help you feel connected with generations of Christians who have come before you and with those who will come after you?

—How does Christ's reign help you to be more loving in your daily living?

—In the times when you may worry about the church's future, what hope do you find in knowing that Christ is leading the church each day?

This book began with a hymn, "I Sing to My Savior." It ends with the promise of the Ascension— that Christ is Lord of all. Luke has shown us throughout the Gospel that Jesus' Way is one of forgiveness, welcome, acceptance, joy, hope and love. These are blessings we receive, and these are blessings God calls us to share. Jesus Christ is our Savior and Lord. In him we have new life— on earth, as one day we will also have new life in heaven.

And so, we as a church gather to sing! Then we as a church sing our way into a hurting world with Jesus' song of love.

Appendix One
Complete List of My Hymns with Luke References

This list includes many hymns that are found in *I Sing to My Savior*— abbreviated "SING" in the list below. It also shows which of my hymns related to Luke's gospel are found in my first two books of hymns: *Gifts of Love: New Hymns for Today's Worship* (Louisville, KY, Geneva Press) - (GL), and from *Songs of Grace: New Hymns for God and Neighbor* (Nashville, TN, Discipleship Resources) - (SG). All of my hymns, including new ones that have been written since this book, can be found on my website: www.carolynshymns.com

Luke 1:26-38: There's Not a Thing That God Can't Do
Luke 1:26-38: The Candle of Hope
Luke 1:26-56, 2:1-20: Mary Heard the Angel's Message - GL
Luke 1:27: God of Generations - GL
Luke 1:39-45: My Soul Proclaims That God is Good
Luke 1:39-55: The Lowly Will Be Lifted Up
Luke 1:39-56: Angel Gabriel Went to Galilee - SING
Luke 1:39-56: Mary Gladly Told Her Cousin - SING
Luke 1:46-55: All the Music Sung and Played Here - SG
Luke 1:46-55: A New Father, Awe-Struck
Luke 1:46-55: God, We See What You Have Given
Luke 1:46-55: How Can It Be (Faithfulness)
Luke 1:46-55: How Can It Be (O Quanta Qualia)
Luke 1:46-55: How Long, O Lord, Will Justice Take?
Luke 1:46-55: I Sing to My Savior - SING
Luke 1:46-55: My Soul Proclaims That God is Good - SING
Luke 1:46-55: My Soul Rejoices in the Lord
Luke 1:46B-55: We Can't Sit On Fences
Luke 1:46b-55: The Candle of Hope
Luke 1:57-79: When Old Zechariah Saw What God Had Done - SING
Luke 1:68-79: The Candle of Hope

Luke 1:79: God of Mercy, You Have Shown Us
Luke 2: In a Feed Box, In a Stable - GL
Luke 2:1-20: A New Father, Awe-Struck
Luke 2:1-20: "Fear Not," The Angel Said - GL
Luke 2:1-20: O God, Your Grace Has Now Appeared - SING
Luke 2:1-20: The Candle of Hope
Luke 2:1-20: When Mary and Joseph Sought Safety and Shelter
Luke 2:1-21: What a World of Sound - GL
Luke 2:7: If I Saw My Toddler
Luke 2:14: The Peace That We Share
Luke 2:19, 2:8-20: When Mary Hugged Her Newborn Son - SING
Luke 2:22-40: A Baby, A Blessing! A Husband and Wife - SING
Luke 2:29-32: Lord, Let Your Servant Go in Peace - SING
Luke 2:41-52: Jesus' Parents Left the Temple - SING
Luke 3:1-6: John Spoke As a Prophet - SING
Luke 3:1-6: O God of Peace, You Sent Us John
Luke 3:1-22: Down By the Jordan - SG
Luke 3:7-18: If I Have Two Coats - SING
Luke 3:7-18: John Proclaimed, "Change your lives!"
Luke 3:7-18: John Proclaimed It: "Change Your Lives!"
Luke 3:7-18: John Went Out to Preach God's Word
Luke 3:15-17: John Was Preaching in the Desert - SING
Luke 3:21-22: John Was Preaching in the Desert
Luke 3:21-22: Spirit of God - GL
Luke 4: Sing Out! Sound the Trumpets! Proclaim Jubilee! -GL - SING
Luke 4:1-13: God, We Long for Our Own Comfort - SING
Luke 4:1-13: Our Lord, You Were Sent - SG
Luke 4:1-13: O Lord, The Spirit Led You
Luke 4:1-13: You Give Your Church a Story
Luke 4:16-19: O God, In Christ You Call Us
Luke 4:18: God, You Alone Know What You've Planned
Luke 4:18-19: God, How Many Are A Thousand? - GL
Luke 4:19: Welcoming God - GL

Luke 9:28-36: O Lord, As You Were On Your Way - SG
Luke 9:43b-45, 9:46-48: Who is Greatest in the Kingdom? - SING
Luke 9:51-62: Should We Call Down Fire from Heaven?
Luke 9:52-56: God of All Peoples
Luke 10:25-37: God, In Our Church's Teaching
Luke 10:25-37: God of Creation - SG
Luke 10:25-37: God, We Thank You For the Churches - SING
Luke 10:25-37: Lord, When Were You in Prison?
Luke 10:25-37: O Christ, We Remember the Things That You Did
Luke 10:25-37: There Is a Time for Silence
Luke 10:25-37: Who Is My Neighbor? - SG -
Luke 10:25-46: O God, You Give Us Neighbors - SING
Luke 10:35-47, 13:29, 14:15-24: There is Room in God's Great Welcome
Luke 10:36-37: O God, In Christ You Call Us
Luke 10:38-42: Martha Labored in the Kitchen - SING
Luke 11:1-13, 18:9-14: When You Are Praying - GL
Luke 11:5-8: O God, May We Keep Praying
Luke 11:13: When Jesus Called You "Father"- SING
Luke 11:33: Like Lamps on the Lamp Stand
Luke 12:13-21: Bigger Barns - SG
Luke 12:13-21: If Only I Had Known
Luke 12:32-48: Don't Fear, Little Flock - SING
Luke 13:1-9: One Day the News was Grim - SING
Luke 13:10-17: That Woman in the Crowd - SING
Luke 13:20-21: Blest are God's Peacemaking Ones - SG
Luke 13:28-40: Two Disciples, Sent by Jesus
Luke 13:29, 14:12-24, 15, 22:14-20, 24:30-31: Christ, You Often Sat at Dinner
Luke 13:29-30: O God, You Love the Needy
Luke 13:31-35: Lord, We Confess We Turn Away - SING
Luke 13:31-35: Since the Lord is My Salvation
Luke 14:12-14: O God, You Love the Needy
Luke 14:15-24: Jesus' Wondrous Words of Grace
Luke 14:16-24: A King Planned a Party - SING

Luke 15: God's Great Love Is So Amazing - GL
Luke 15: Jesus' Wondrous Words of Grace - SING
Luke 15: O God, In Your Love - GL
Luke 15: Welcoming God - GL
Luke 15:1: God of All Peoples
Luke 15:1-3, 15:11b-32: The Prodigal Son - SING
Luke 15:1-3,11b-32: We're Part of the Blessing
Luke 15:2, 17:11-19, 7:1-10: Christ, You Are The Savior - SING
Luke 15:11-32: When Jesus Called You "Father"
Luke 15:11-32: When Jesus Went to Egypt
Luke 16:1-15: A Dishonest Steward - SING
Luke 16:19-31: God, We Build Our Own Divisions
Luke 16:19-31: If Only I Had Known
Luke 16:19-31: Outside My Gate, Outside My Door - SING
Luke 16:19-31: Through Devastating Storms
Luke 17:11-19: Ten Who Suffered Sought Out Jesus - SING
Luke 18:1-8: God, You Hear Our Weary Praying - SING
Luke 18:1-8: O God, May We Keep Praying
Luke 18:9-14: A Pharisee Was Praying - SING
Luke 18:15-17: Do Not Turn Away the Children
Luke 18:15-17: When Children Scream from Tear Gas
Luke 18:15-17: When We Watch the Rescue
Luke 18:18-30: Lord, What Must I Do? - SING
Luke 18:18-30: One Day As Jesus Was Traveling Through
Luke 19:1-10: Welcoming God - GL
Luke 19:1-10: Zacchaeus Was a Tax Man - SING
Luke 19:12-27: Jesus, Have Mercy! - SING
Luke 19:12-27: O God, We Yearn for Safety - SING
Luke 19:28-40: Lord, What a Parade! - SING
Luke 19:28-40: One Day as Jesus Reached a Town
Luke 19:37-44: O God, the Things That Make for Peace
Luke 19:38-40: We Long to Know Peace!
Luke 19:41: The Peace That We Share
Luke 19:45-48: When Christ Went to the Temple - SING
Luke 20:17: God, When You Called Our Church by Grace
Luke 20:20-26: Is It Lawful to Pay Taxes? - SING

Appendix Two
Helpful Resources on the Gospel of Luke

Bailey, Kenneth E. *Jesus Through Middle Eastern Eyes: Cultural Studies in the Gospels*, Downers Grove, IL: IVP Academic Press, 2008.

Bailey, Kenneth E. *Poet & Peasant and Through Peasant Eyes: A Literary-Cultural Approach to the Parables in Luke.* Grand Rapids, MI: Eerdmans, 1983.

Carroll, John T. *Luke: A Commentary (The New Testament Library),* Louisville, KY: Westminster John Knox Press, 2015.

Craddock, Fred B. *Luke (Interpretation: A Bible Commentary for Teaching and Preaching).* Louisville, KY: Westminster John Knox Press, 1990.

Crowder, Stephanie Buckhannon "Luke" in *True to Our Native Land: An African American New Testament Commentary* edited by Brian K. Blount, Cain Hope Felder, Clarice Martin, Minneapolis, MN: Fortress, 2007.

Culpepper, R. Alan "The Gospel of Luke," *The New Interpreter's Bible*, Volume IX. Nashville, TN: Abingdon Press, 1995.

Gench, Frances Taylor. *Back to the Well: Women's Encounters with Jesus in the Gospels.* Louisville, KY: Westminster John Knox Press, 2004.

González, Justo L. González. *Luke (Belief: A Theological Commentary on the Bible).* Louisville, KY: Westminster John Knox Press, 2010.

Green, Joel B. *The Gospel of Luke (The New International Commentary on the New Testament)*. Grand Rapids, MI: Eerdmans, 1997.

Jarvis, Cynthia A. and Johnson, Elizabeth E. *Feasting on the Gospels--Luke, Volumes 1 & 2: A Feasting on the Word Commentary.* Louisville, KY: Westminster John Knox Press, 2014.

Karris, Robert J. *A Symphony of New Testament Hymns.* Collegeville, MN: Liturgical Press, 1996.

Levine, Amy-Jill and Witherington III, Ben. *The Gospel of Luke (New Cambridge Bible Commentary).* New York: Cambridge University Press, 2018.

Ringe, Sharon H. *Luke (Westminster Bible Companion).* Louisville, KY: Westminster John Knox Press, 1995

Schaberg Jane D. & Ringe, Sharon H. "Gospel of Luke," *Women's Bible Commentary* Third Edition, edited by Carol A. Newsom, Sharon H. Ringe, Jacqueline E. Lapsley. Louisville, KY: Westminster John Knox Press, 2012.

Wright, N.T. *Luke for Everyone (The New Testament for Everyone)* Louisville, KY: Westminster John Knox Press, 2004.

ABOUT THE AUTHOR

Carolyn Winfrey Gillette has been a pastor in rural, small town, suburban, and city churches; she has also served as a hospice chaplain, a hospital chaplain, and a school bus aide helping children with special needs.

Carolyn is a gifted hymn writer who has written over 400 hymns. These hymns have been sung by congregations throughout the United States and around the world— from the Washington National Cathedral to St. Giles' Cathedral in Edinburgh, Scotland, to small town churches and small household congregations; they have also been sung at national church and international ecumenical meetings.

In addition to *I Sing to My Savior*, she has written *Gifts of Love: New Hymns for Today's* Worship (Geneva Press) and *Songs of Grace: New Hymns for God and Neighbor* (Upper Room Books). Her hymns have been published in over 20 books. Two of her hymns have been published by the Choristers Guild as anthems. Carolyn was commissioned to write the lead article for the special issue on "Singing Our Lives" for Baylor University's *Christian Reflection* journal. Her hymns have also been in *Call to Worship* journal, *The Chorister* (cover story), *Reformed Worship, The Presbyterian Outlook* and on thousands of web sites. All of her hymns can be found on her website with indices to scriptural references, topics, tunes, and the three-year cycle of the Revised Common Lectionary: www.carolynshymns.com

The World Council of Churches, National Council of Churches, Church World Service and Churches Uniting in Christ have asked her to write hymns. Habitat for Humanity International used a hymn by Carolyn for their 30th anniversary celebration. Family Promise (Interfaith Hospitality Network) did a music video of her hymn for their ministry with homeless families. The Humane Society of the United States did a music video contest of her hymn for their Blessing of the Animals service. The Presbyterian Church (USA) 216th General Assembly presented her with the "Ecumenical and Interreligious Service Recognition." *Sojourners* did a short video about her hymn writing. A Canadian scholar wrote her biography for the *Cambridge Dictionary for Hymnology*.

Feature stories about Carolyn's hymns addressing concerns facing the Church, nation and world, were done by *The New Yorker, Christian Century, America, National Public Radio,* national *PBS-TV,* and newspapers (*Philadelphia Inquirer, Washington Post, Courier Post, News Journal,* and others).

Carolyn is a graduate of Lebanon Valley College and Princeton Theological Seminary. She finds joy in parish ministry, hymn writing, and most of all in her family as a wife, mother (and foster mother), grandmother, sister, and human parent to a rescue dog, "Annie."

Carolyn sees her hymn writing as a partnership and is very grateful for prayers for her hymn writing, suggestions for hymns, gifts for hymn use and commissions, and invitations to speak at conferences, workshops, and church gatherings (in person and online). She hopes her hymns nurture people in their discipleship and support churches in their worship and service in the world. Sing to the Lord a new song!

Made in the USA
Middletown, DE
05 August 2022